The Spirit of the Cotswolds

ALSO BY SUSAN HILL

The Spirit of the
Cotswolds

Susan Hill

with photographs by
Nick Meers

A MERMAID BOOK

Author's note to second and subsequent impressions

Some of the information and details in the text have inevitably changed since the book was researched and written during 1987.

MICHAEL JOSEPH LTD
Published by the Penguin Group
27 Wrights Lane, London W8 5TZ, England
Viking Penguin Inc., 40 West 23rd Street, New York, New York 10010, USA
Penguin Books Australia Ltd, Ringwood, Victoria, Australia
Penguin Books Canada Ltd, 2801 John Street, Markham, Ontario, Canada L3R 1B4
Penguin Books (NZ) Ltd, 182-190 Wairau Road, Auckland 10, New Zealand

Penguin Books Ltd, Registered Offices: Harmondsworth, Middlesex, England.

First published May 1988
Second impression October 1988
First published in Mermaid Books March 1990

Text Copyright © Susan Hill, 1988
Photographs Copyright © Nick Meers, 1988

Filmset in 11/13 Imprint by Goodfellow & Egan Ltd, Cambridge
Printed and bound in Italy by L.E.G.O.

A CIP catalogue record for this book is available from the British Library
ISBN hardback 0 7181 2905 9
paperback 0 7181 3299 8

page 1: *Coln Valley near Chedworth*
page 2-3: *Broadway tower seen from near Buckland*
page 4-5: *Early morning near Charlton Abbots*

Contents

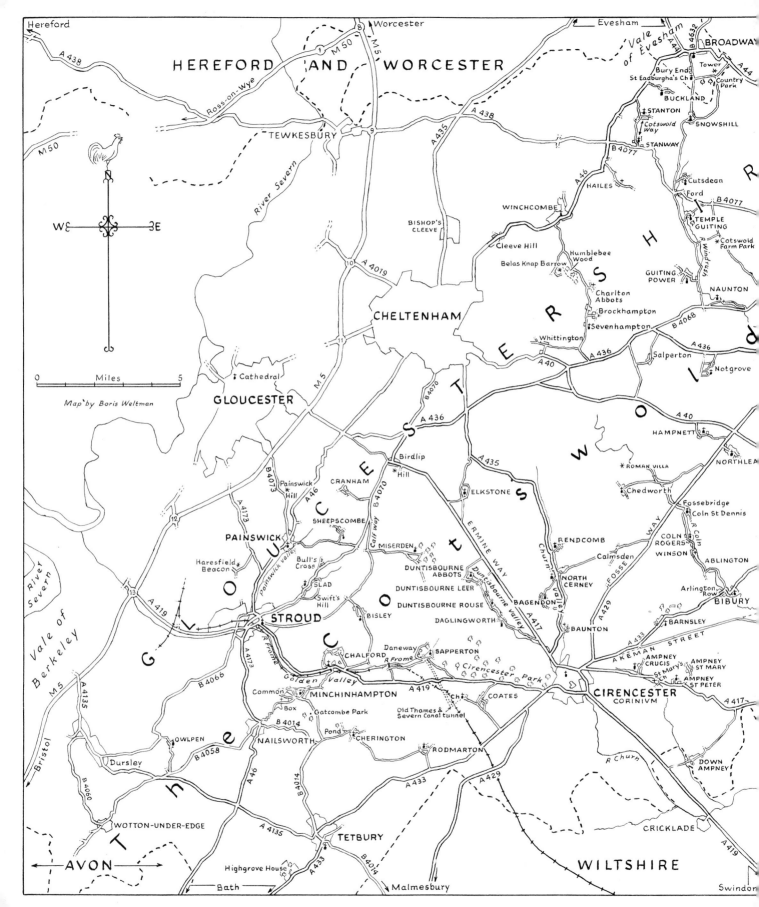

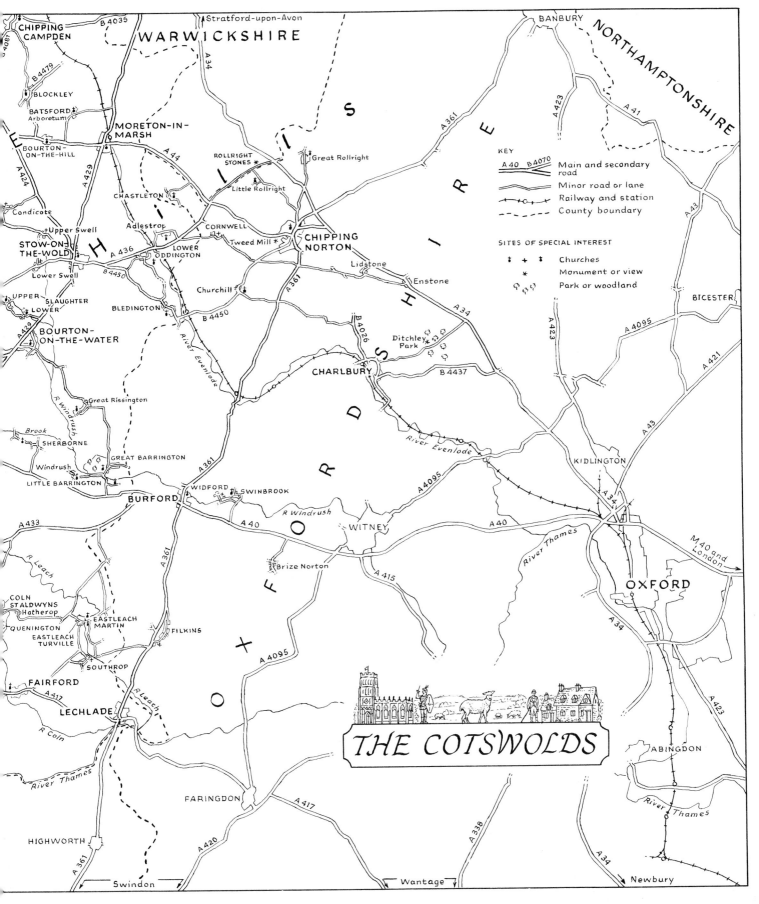

THE COTSWOLDS

KEY

A 40   B 4070 — Main and secondary road

Minor road or lane

Railway and station

County boundary

SITES OF SPECIAL INTEREST

✝ ✝ ✝   Churches

✳   Monument or view

🌳 🌳🌳   Park or woodland

WARWICKSHIRE

NORTHAMPTONSHIRE

OXFORDSHIRE

CHIPPING CAMPDEN
BLOCKLEY
BATSFORD Arboretum
MORETON-IN-MARSH
BOURTON-ON-THE-HILL
Condicote
Upper Swell
STOW-ON-THE-WOLD
Lower Swell
UPPER SLAUGHTER
LOWER
BOURTON-ON-THE-WATER
CHASTLETON
Adlestrop
LOWER ODDINGTON
CORNWELL
Tweed Mill
ROLLRIGHT STONES
Great Rollright
Little Rollright
CHIPPING NORTON
Lidstone
Enstone
Churchill
BLEDINGTON
Great Rissington
R Windrush
Brook
SHERBORNE
Windrush
GREAT BARRINGTON
LITTLE BARRINGTON
WIDFORD
SWINBROOK
BURFORD
Ditchley Park
CHARLBURY
River Evenlode
River Evenlode
KIDLINGTON
BICESTER
WITNEY
Brize Norton
R Windrush
River Thames
OXFORD
M 40 and London
R Leach
COLN ST ALDWYNS
Hatherop
QUENINGTON
EASTLEACH TURVILLE
EASTLEACH MARTIN
FILKINS
SOUTHROP
FAIRFORD
LECHLADE
R Leach
R Coln
River Thames
FARINGDON
HIGHWORTH
ABINGDON
River Thames
Swindon
Wantage
Newbury

Stratford-upon-Avon
BANBURY

B 4035
B 4479
B 4081
A 429
A 424
A 44
A 436
B 4450
A 429
B 4450
B 4026
A 361
A 34
A 423
A 41
A 43
A 4095
A 421
A 423
B 4437
A 4095
A 40
A 415
A 40
A 34
A 34
A 433
A 361
A 4095
A 417
A 417
A 420
A 338
A 423
A 34
A 361

WOLDS

1. The Spirit of the Cotswolds

I spent almost a year journeying through the Cotswold region, from the end of one December to the beginning of the next, for the purpose of writing this book. I went alone, with my husband, with a friend, and in the company of my family. I spent hours gazing about me, I walked in the country, I pottered about in the high streets of market towns and in the back lanes of villages. I listened, shopped locally, stayed in pubs and hotels, mingled with the everyday scene. I read a great many books and local newspapers, too; I pored over Ordnance Survey maps, but above all I looked, and I thought, and let myself be receptive to the spirit of the Cotswolds which I knew was there – knew I would recognise when it touched me. I didn't know what it was exactly – and I still do not. Like the Holy Spirit, the spirit of any region 'bloweth where it listeth'. When I confidently expected to find it, I did not; and then I would turn a corner, all unthinking, and meet it head on.

It is an atmosphere, and it is also something visual – visual perfection, I think, when a place is utterly right in every aspect, when architecture, building material, overall layout fit their setting in such a way that you cannot imagine any change, cannot see them anywhere else. And if you imagine the landscape before the buildings were put there, you are imagining something incomplete, the setting minus the jewel. It is when the buildings and the landscape are in a particular mood, too, which has to do with season, weather, quality, intensity and play of light. Yet chocolate-box perfection, over-preserved or restored perfection are wrong; you may find the past frozen in amber in the Cotswolds, but the spirit will be absent, there will be a deadness that you can sense, an artificiality.

The spirit of the Cotswolds is a living thing; it has to do with people and their activities – the rightness of

a street full of shoppers on market day; a tractor crossing a nut-brown field with the furrow unfurling like a seam behind it; a line of riders along the crest of a hill or a party of ramblers trudging along the Cotswold Way; an old man in trousers and waistcoat, shirt and hat and boots, with a pipe but without a jacket, hoeing, scritch-scratch along the line of potatoes in his kitchen garden; a publican pulling a pint in a dark, cool, oak-panelled bar; a wedding party, a funeral group, a gaggle of schoolchildren at the Corinium Museum and another among the animals at the Cotswold Farm Park. And coach loads of Americans peering out at Broadway and Bibury and Lower Slaughter, and half the holidaymakers of England eating ice creams in Bourton-on-the-Water.

For above all, the Cotswolds are a region of contrast,

(Opposite) *View towards Bourton-on-the-Water;*
(right) *Cotswold barns, Salperton*

and contrast in landscape, first and foremost. It is an area of infinite variety, and the dramatic changes take place within a very few miles. About the only thing they do not have is the sea – though stand on Birdlip Hill looking over to Gloucester, and the blue line of the Severn is the tongue that runs down into the mouth of it.

I have felt extraordinarily satisfied in my craving for all kinds of landscape; for heights, as Cleeve Hill, Painswick Hill or beside Broadway Tower, below which the country lies and you feel you could take wings and fly, soar down over the plain, above the 'coloured counties', the stone villages, the green and brown fields.

Best of all, I love the wild windswept lonely Cotswold uplands, grassy places where sheep are scattered like mushrooms all about, and the dry stone walls cross like braid in all directions. There is the same sense of bleak isolation, the same eerie whistling of the wind, the same cold air that you have on the moors of the North of England. Stand alone on one of these uplands, and the spirit of the Cotswolds will blow towards you on

View from Birdlip Hill, looking towards Gloucester

the cry of the sheep and the birds, but if you run after it, it will bob ahead of you, always just out of reach.

Down from the uplands run the deep, wooded clefts and there is a secretiveness in these places; it is always cool and still and damp, always quiet but never silent. Then, in the lee of the ridge huddle the little golden villages in which you find warmth and shelter and a different sort of seclusion.

You move very quickly from complete isolation and emptiness to busy roads, from small, empty villages to tourist towns; escape is always easily possible, from the crowds or from alone-ness, from the chill wind or the closeness of the low-lying places beside the rivers. There are handsome buildings and pretty, cosy, chintzy buildings; small picture-book cottages set individually or built in rows, and elegant manor houses, and always the stone, and every stone of that stone a subtly different shade of the same narrow range of colours. And everywhere, the churches.

Surely, if the spirit of the Cotswolds resides any-where, it must be in the churches: small, bare and exquisite ones like Duntisbourne Rouse or Hailes; eccentric ones like St Kenelm at Sapperton; self-important wool churches, welcoming churches full of parish life, redundant churches, churches smelling of damp and cold, cold stone, of must and neglect and decay. No, until you open the door of a church and walk in, you cannot tell whether it will be plain or ornate, cluttered or bare, beautiful or ugly, and you cannot tell until you stand in it, look around it, breathe in it, read the notices, pray in it, whether the spirit does indeed dwell here, whether it has a living heart or a dead, shrivelled, desiccated one.

Whether you respond to a church is, in great part, a

(Opposite top) *Upland view near Condicote. Cotswold houses: cottages at Calmsden* (opposite bottom) *and manor house in the Slad Valley (right)*

matter of visual preference, religious inclination, taste. Virtually every church has its individual treasures and there is nothing you do not find somewhere in the region.

On my journeying, I made favourites, fell in love with particular churches – often for no tangible, stateable reason; I love Baunton for its wall-painting, and Hailes for its holiness, Sapperton for its situation, Chipping Campden for its tower, Elkstone and Duntisbourne Abbots for the churchyards, and St Oswald's, Widford, for its isolation in among the water meadows. I have been touched closely by a sense of the past, at Bagendon, at Swinbrook and at Ampney St Mary, moved by the powerful emotion expressed on individual memorials, touched to the heart by the epitaphs on gravestones; and felt peace in the cloisters of Gloucester Cathedral, and awe and reverence such as I have not often felt in my life, looking up at the great glass windows of Fairford.

Other churches have left me cold and the reasons are as much to do with me as with the buildings. Everyone who visits the Cotswold churches must let them speak and listen for the response within themselves. Where I have found the spirit, others will not. What is it about that most precious of churches to me, St Nicholas at Lower Oddington? Why does the spirit of the Cotswolds live in the blackbirds darting low on the ground in among the yew trees in Painswick churchyard?

When I began to visit the Cotswolds, I expected to be able to see them with a certain amount of detachment, for on the whole, I have no particular personal connection with them, although I live on their borders,

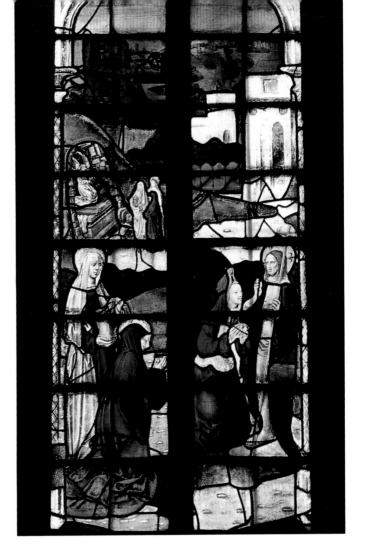

(Opposite top) *St Kenelm, Sapperton;* (opposite bottom) *the churchyards of St Peter, Duntisbourne Abbots and St John, Elkstone.* (Above right) *One of the windows at St Mary, Fairford*

and they do not belong to my own past but are very much part of the present.

Instead, I found myself undertaking a series of interconnected journeys which took on something of the nature of a pilgrimage, and my responses to the region became intensely personal and emotional. What I have written about them reflects this, and is in many ways an idiosyncratic vision of the Cotswolds, but landscape is not a fixed and static thing, an object to be viewed from without; it is living, changing, growing, a part of history, a part of the present, and landscape, place, affects people and inter-reacts with them and the way they live their lives. What happens to us domestically, socially, emotionally, affects our view of the places in which it happens, and the setting becomes tinged with our own individual experience.

Travelling through the Cotswolds, I have been very aware of other people, ordinary people, from the past and in the present, and of the imprint they have left on the landscape, the way they have shaped together the region in which they have lived and worked, and the way they continue to do so. And because the Cotswolds is a tourist region and, like many other beautiful and historic parts of the British Isles, will become increasingly so as tourism fast becomes one of our major industries, it is as much the people who visit the region, who pass through it on foot, by road or by rail, for a day or a week, who affect and help to change it. In them, too, it provokes a response, awakens feelings, causes changes of thought, awareness, vision. The interaction between people and place is a continuing and developing one.

The region grew on the backs of the sheep who grazed it. Merchants got rich as the sheep got heavy with their wool, and they spent their money on providing themselves with remarkably handsome and comfortable manor houses – many of which still stand – and on endowing the region with a great many beautiful churches, in gratitude and piety. The more philanthropic among them also built and endowed almshouses, hospitals and schools, and cottages for their dependants, tenants and estate workers.

But where there are rich landlords, there will also be a few bad landlords, as well as those who exploit those who work for them. The history of the Cotswolds is, in part, the history of generations of anonymous, unskilled labourers who endured short lives of hard work in all weathers for little reward. So it has always been, and not, of course, only in the Cotswolds.

During the early years of this century, and after the Second World War, there were still prosperous landowners but many lords of the manor found it a hard struggle to keep up large houses and estates. Cottages were neglected and land sold off, many a beautiful manor house disintegrated into a sorry state of disrepair. There have always been farmers – sheep, arable and dairy – in the Cotswolds, but not by any means all of them have made a fat living off the land.

In the last few years, prosperity has come to the Cotswolds again, and even over the year during which I have been writing, demand for manor houses and cottages has been insatiable, and house prices have rocketed. With improved road and rail communications, some people are prepared to commute to London; others, often the self-employed, have sold their London houses at enormous profit and moved into the country where, for the price of a small Victorian house in Putney, they can – or rather, they could until recently

– buy a six-bedroomed Cotswold stone manor house with an acre of land in a beautiful village. The result is visible all over the region. The new- or in-comers have bought up property which may have been long neglected, and they have money to restore it – or, if they are going about it with more money than sensitivity, 'do it up'. Of course, many of the long-established local people are still there – those born in the Cotswolds and who have lived and worked here all their lives.

But the villages are also full of prosperous middle-class families from elsewhere with expensive cars, several children and a paddock full of ponies. Spare money to buy smart clothes and high-quality provisions has encouraged shop-keepers to open in the market towns. There is evidence of a new, rather brash prosperity – and a rash of builders, everywhere. You cannot go into a village without finding a barn being converted to a luxury executive dwelling, a field being filled up with 'cottage-style retirement homes', a cottage being re-thatched, extended, given a double garage.

As a result, jobs have been created locally for innumerable skilled craftsmen and allied workers, and so the prosperity extends sideways, and more and more people have disposable income. Road traffic increases, towns and villages are busier; and in the major tourist centres, numerous houses and shops are given over specifically to cater for their needs, thus attracting ever more visitors – the honeypot syndrome. Compare all this to postcards and photographs of even just twenty years ago, and the whole look of the area is different.

I have on my desk a small descriptive book about the Cotswolds, first published in 1930, and long out of print. It welcomes the fact that 'the charm and peace of most of the beautiful old Cotswold villages have

Ripe for development? (Top) *Barn near Bibury;* (centre) *Oathill Barn near Rodmarton;* (bottom) *Keble Barn at Coln St Aldwyns – the notice of a planning application is already posted on the gate*

been saved from spoliation and disturbance by the unwelcome presence of the railway', and goes on to say, 'there are *some* people, no doubt, who can find an element of the picturesque in a railway line or a railway train.'

Oh, indeed, and I am assuredly one of them. There is a romance in railway trains that has never belonged to the motor car, a charm in the country station found nowhere else. But the writer of that book would feel even happier nowadays, since even the relatively few

Near Brookthorpe, with Haresfield Beacon beyond

branch lines that used to cross the Cotswold region have long disappeared. There is a decent main line that passes through the Cotswolds en route from Hereford to London and, recently, the service has been speeded up and improved out of all recognition, which has encouraged more businessmen to become long-distance commuters. And you can get from Cheltenham to Gloucester, and thence to London; and that's about all.

But the same writer would find her predictions about motor traffic sadly out of line. 'Motor coaches run to the principal towns on the high roads and to other accessible places, but even those ubiquitous

vehicles cannot penetrate into those delectable corners where Cotswold hides its greatest charms.'

Alas, they can, and they do, and they have spoiled many quiet corners, ruined certain towns and villages irretrievably. The main roads of the Cotswolds, as those anywhere else in the British Isles, are fast, crowded roads, carrying monstrously heavy lorries as well as tourist coaches, and a huge volume of private cars. They are a pollution, and most of all, a *visual* scar on the landscape – rows of parked cars down beautiful streets, market squares crammed with them, spoiling the line of the buildings; the grace and beauty of individual houses and cottages are blotted out by them, even the precincts of cathedrals have bowed down before their demands. If the motor car is not tamed and controlled, it will choke the Cotswolds to death. The area is still best seen by those on foot or on horseback, and is much traversed by both.

If variety and contrast are the hallmarks of the Cotswolds, they are as evident in the type of people who live and work there as in the landscape. There are the rich – indeed, many of the *very* rich; there is some 'old' money still, a few titled landowners, but far more who have come new to wealth and the possession of old stone manor houses and all the trappings of success – businessmen, financiers, entrepreneurs, pop stars; there are the Royals and their attendant courtiers.

There are independent farmers, struggling tenant farmers, cottagers, farm workers. And, because there is a certain amount of light industry and technology, particularly towards Gloucester in the west of the region, there are ordinary working people, young couples with young children filling the shopping streets and supermarkets on Saturday afternoons, with only a slight Gloucestershire accent to distinguish them as Cotswold dwellers from similar people anywhere else in the country. And standing about on street corners, in the towns, are plenty of the new young men, macho-looking, slightly sinister, accompanied by big aggressive dogs on very short leads.

Lane leading away from St Nicholas, Lower Oddington

(Left) *River Coln at Coln Rogers;* (above) *farmland seen from Swift's Hill in the Slad Valley*

In the villages there are still a few 'characters', old men of the soil who have rarely been outside the county all their lives. But they are a dying breed.

Among the visitors you see variety, too: the up-market tourists, often American, stay in the expensive country-house hotels and tour the Cotswolds in hired limousines. The ice-cream visitors have gaggles of children and rarely leave the main tourist towns; the rest rarely leave their air-conditioned coaches.

But I have to say that in all my recent journeys in the Cotswolds, people have impinged upon me very little. For however many there are, even in high summer, it is always easy to escape from them and go somewhere else to be quite alone. And, more important, the whole great landscape of the Cotswolds, its past, and all the things it contains, is infinitely greater than the people, it takes over and dwarfs them, no matter how much impact they may apparently be making upon it.

The people I have been most aware of have been the dead: the ghosts of the early English in the earth of the prehistoric burial mounds, of the Dobunni at Bagendon, of the Roman armies marching across country; at Lower Oddington and Ampney St Mary, I have thought of all the poor victims of the Black Death, so suddenly swept away; the dead have lain quietly beneath my feet in innumerable graveyards, and I have read their names on tombs, been moved by the brief details of their tragedies, looked up and seen their effigies on imposing marble or slate monuments.

At every barn, every stone wall, every cottage, every manor, every church, I have heard the whispering voices of all the anonymous workmen, the stonemasons and carpenters, thatchers and tilers; and in the churches especially generations of the silent dead come alive as I have gloried in what they have made and left behind them – the wall paintings, the stone carvings on fonts, pulpits and over doorways, the mighty windows. At Hailes Abbey, and in the cloisters at Gloucester, I have stood in silence and heard the monks, long dead but who still sing, still pray. The region is steeped in Christianity, inspiring the men who built, carved, painted, worshipped, lived and died declaring it, it shaped the look of every village and every town in the region.

But go into any village church at Christmas, at Easter, at the time of Harvest Festival, after a wedding or a baptism or a funeral, and you will know that although men may no longer be building in stone to the greater glory of God, the religion that inspired their Cotswold predecessors is still a living thing and not merely part of history. Read the messages in any of the dozens of visitors' books in the churches, and you understand that it is something that the visitors share in and take home with them. Their comments reveal what they value most about these buildings – the peace and quietness, the sense of the past, the beauty of the stone, the atmosphere that inspires awe and reverence, and the fact that the churches and their artefacts continue to stand as symbolic offerings of praise and places of prayer and worship in an unbroken line down the centuries.

And I suppose, finally, that is what I have been most strongly aware of during all my journeying in the Cotswolds – the sense of the past, in the middle of the present, the inextricable intermingling of yesterday and today.

The English regions have produced many a fine poet to sing their praises – but one of the finest and most poignant, as well as the least well known, is Ivor Gurney whose poems, written from the trenches of the First World War, are full of aching thoughts of his home Cotswolds.

An odd stanza, a single line or image here and there, encapsulates and evokes not just his own region of Gloucestershire, but the whole of the countryside of which the Cotswolds are the heart, and in which you will always find the spirit which is the spirit of the English rural countryside.

The orchis, trefoil, harebells nod all day,
High above Gloucester and the Severn Plain.
Few come there, where the curlew ever and again
Cries faintly, and no traveller makes stay,
Since steep the road is,
And the villages
Hidden by hedges wonderful in May.

It was scarcely surprising that a young poet in the trenches of that terrible war should look back in longing to England and his Gloucestershire home. After my own happy year journeying in the Cotswolds, I know that if I were sent into any sort of exile, I should now feel the same. Any visitor to the region will quickly come to understand why. Any Cotswold native will do so already.

Near Bourton-on-the-Water

2. Chipping Norton

I never take a major road if I can avoid it. I have been all over the Cotswolds – as indeed, I have been in many another area of the British Isles – by the most winding, wayward and idiosyncratic of routes. And I can't think of any disadvantages of going by the back roads, so long as you are not in a hurry and you don't mind being occasionally stuck behind a farm wagon for a few miles. Indeed, going at 15 miles per hour behind a tractor gives you a chance to peer through gaps in the hedges, and down tracks and up driveways, and that is, above all, the way to discover all the secret places of the Cotswolds that hide everywhere, like all the tiny creatures that hide down deep in the ditch, unnoticed by the speeding traveller.

Wherever a main road is unavoidable, I am miserable and nervous, poring over the map to find the nearest point at which I can dive down some tiny lane which will take us approximately in the direction we want to go, albeit in twice the time. For it is via the minor roads, the country lanes, that you penetrate to the heart of the area, and discover that it is unspoilt after all, unspoilt and peaceful and often empty, so that you can be half a mile from a busy trunk road, stop the car beside a gate, still the engine and get out – and hear only the susurration of the wind in the leaves of a nearby copse, the thin song of a lark spiralling upwards above the cornfield, the pip-pip-pip of some tiny bird hidden deep in the hedge. No voices, no engines.

The Bliss Valley Tweed Mill at Chipping Norton

My home village lies five miles to the east of the City of Oxford. Although it has so many of the essential Cotswold ingredients in its little lanes, stone cottages glimpsed down garden paths, and the four-square handsome church with its medieval wall painting, it is truly an Oxfordshire village.

The way I like to let myself into the Cotswolds is, as it were, by the back door, easing my way in quietly. It is the very best way to arrive there. I head off the busy A.34 Oxford to Stratford-upon-Avon road as soon as possible, and take the straight, single-track across the flat fields beside Ditchley Park, in the direction of Charlbury, a road so obscure that it is missing from a good many maps, and we always get lost at some point or other every time we take it, but we never fail to find something of delight either. The last time we went, it was a glorious morning in May, unseasonably hot, and we were taking a family day out, as we do several times a year, in the parts of the Cotswolds that lie nearest to our Oxfordshire home: we did not meet one other car, or any sign of human life, until we drove into the town of Charlbury.

Just beyond the drive that leads to Ditchley, where the road swings left, we stopped and I got out. The air was full of the bleating of ewes and their lambs, and the incessant call of the cuckoo, of a dozen cuckoos; it seemed that they had carved up the countryside between them for miles around. And then, quite suddenly out of nowhere, one appeared and sat upon a post a yard away, a surprisingly large bird, and handsome enough to make you forget and forgive him his nasty habits. And in the woods on either side, all the other birds of Oxfordshire, in full throat. The air was thick with pollen, the heady smell of the sun-yellow rape slashing the country to right and left, exotic in your nostrils, the pungent cow parsley and grass heads, dusty-sweet along the verge. We saw pheasants too, and a partridge, and jays flitting in and out of the trees, and any number of young rabbits,

A temporary delay in a narrow lane

careering into the path of the car, and crazily back again, wild-eyed and bob-tailed.

We drove on, and the sky was as blue as a thrush's egg and Oxfordshire was at her lush, leafy, undulating best – and definitely still Oxfordshire. Through Charlbury, a large village-cum-small market town, old in the centre, but with new estates spreading out all around – a commuter place, and slightly smart. People from London weekend in Charlbury; it has character, it has a real and thriving community life, and a railway station on the Cotswold line that leads up to Worcester and Hereford from Paddington. It has too much motor traffic and a curious one-way street system, and a cricket pitch set to great advantage in the lee of the town. And it is still, indubitably, in Oxfordshire.

So, perhaps because of its very name, is the village of Churchill further on, with its handsome church tower looming up as the road rises to meet it. And in all the hedgerows as we passed, we saw the hawthorn, in ribbons of pink and white, and smelt the incomparable smell of it through the open windows, one of the smells most redolent of my childhood.

Beyond Churchill, on the B.4450 that winds eventually into the true, eastern Cotswolds, is the village of Bledington, and Bledington has, as it were, a foot in either camp, it exactly straddles the invisible border. Its plain, four-square, stone houses and cottages that fringe its large rectangular green are of Cotswold stone and style. Yet something is not quite right, it still has a look of the Oxfordshire places we have just come through.

But wherever it belongs, Bledington is a good place, worth stopping in and wandering around, because it

Spring lamb

has so many of the ingredients which go towards making a harmonious whole, and which might have led to its being exploited and over-run by the tourist traffic. But it is not. Visitors visit, but you do not see Bledington in any of the popular gazetteers of the Cotswolds, and unless you drove by chance down this B road, you would not find it. But perhaps today nowhere remains undiscovered.

On that May morning, the people about in Bledington, apart from ourselves, were local people. Outside the post office, a trio of ladies, chatting with shopping baskets; in the vicinity of the village hall, cars stopping and unloading, and in the open doorway, ladies in aprons, moving tables, preparing a spread.

Bledington does not only have its good, wide village green; it has a stream running through it, crossed by a couple of little flat bridges, and a sub-stream that branches off and then peters out into nothing between grassy banks. And it is this stream that tips the balance in favour of Bledington's belonging to the Cotswolds, rather than not, for villages with small rivers and streams running through the centre of them, villages with splashy fords to be crossed, and gurgling brooks at the bottom of gardens, are dotted everywhere about the region. Bledington has moorhens, and ducks that sit on the grass with their heads swivelled round and tucked down into their back feathers, apparently asleep – until my small daughter bears down upon them, and they uncurl and waddle off smartly, and plop down into the safety of the stream.

On the far side of the green, seven children aged seven or so swung peaceably on the village swings, all out of order with one another, and the swings creaked, and all around, in bushes and hedges, the birds sang and sang.

I like Bledington. Our daughters bought iced lollipops from the village stores, and we sat on a bench and admired the modest houses, all in proportion, and the mossy roofs, and the calm and order of the place; it is neat but not too neat.

If you were feeling energetic, you would leave the car here now, and take a footpath across the fields, to the place you should see next. It isn't far, and the track would be the quietest, gentlest approach, entirely fitting your destination. It is always a mistake to come upon places suddenly, the contrast is too abrupt. Don't go by air if you can go by boat and train, don't drive if you can ride, on cycle or horse, but best of all, simply walk. A counsel of perfection.

But if you do take the car out of Bledington, a mile or two down the B.4450 going north, you will come upon signposts that leave you in no doubt at all that you are now in the Cotswolds. To the west lies Stow-on-the-Wold, and north of that, Moreton-in-

The village green, Bledington

Marsh; to the south-west is Bourton-on-the-Water. But for now, there is somewhere else to go to. It is so close to those familiar names of the tourist haunts, and yet I don't think many people know it, though it is sometimes mentioned in guide-books. It is called Oddington – Lower and Upper.

And when we reached it on that beautiful Saturday morning, we ran right into the middle of a wedding, and became so tangled up in be-ribboned cars and top-hatted gentlemen and ladies swathed in silk and net and flowers and feathers, that we fled, reversing in confusion down the narrowest of lanes to let the carriage folk go past. In the main village street, people stood at their gates and hung out of their windows, and old ladies leaned upon cottage doorposts and even dogs looked up to view the bride, and there was only time for me to say that it was a perfect day to be married on, when we were out, onto the main road and away to market.

It was not until we returned and the place was empty again at the end of a long hot afternoon, when the May sunshine was still bright but the breeze was a little cool, that I could reflect at leisure that this was not just a perfect day, but the most perfect place, for a wedding.

For Oddington is one of the most pleasing, tucked-away villages in the Cotswolds, and it has one of the most beautiful, memorable, and isolated of churches. It is to here, the church of St Nicholas, that you had really far better walk from Bledington, across the field path. That way, its separateness from the village, and its perfect situation, set amidst the mature surrounding trees, and above all its absolute quietness, is discovered best of all.

If you approach the church by car, never mind though, for that way you will come through the narrow streets of the village, and they are shady and secluded, with rows of small, stone, terraced houses. Turn right, following the small signpost to the church, and you feel as if you are leaving civilisation behind again; once, this church of St Nicholas was at the centre of life in Oddington, until the Black Death, that dark disrupter of medieval English life, took most of the people away, and the village was razed and rebuilt on higher, drier, healthier ground that half-mile away. The old church was abandoned. By 1852, it was derelict. The community grew up again and thrived in its new village, and they built another church too. Not until 1912 did restoration of the church of St Nicholas begin.

Tomb in the churchyard of St Nicholas, Oddington

14th-century Doom wall-painting in St Nicholas

Now, apart from its isolation, you would not know that the world had turned its back on the medieval church. It has been meticulously restored and it is lovingly cared for, and there is no feeling of lifelessness or newness nor any air of artificial preservation about it. I like it as well as any other country church in the Cotswolds.

We walked up the sloping path towards the porch, and in the shade of the trees it was cool. The graveyard forms a square, and the grass was uncut but somehow not untidy – I hate shaven churchyards. Around the sides, a low dry-stone wall, and then the tall trees, thickly leaved now, and rippling a little, to let the sunshine fall in changing patterns onto the grass and the gravestones. The children plunged off amongst

them, to climb and clamber and step high between the stalks of sorrel and plantain heads, and I thought, as I've often thought, that all churchyards should have children to play in them from time to time. It is a good thing to mingle together the vigorously living and the peaceful dead.

Then I went into the church. It was dark and cool after the sunshine outside, but Oddington church has no stained glass so the light that comes through the windows is clear and pale. I don't care for most stained glass, unless it is as wonderful – and rare – as the medieval glass of Fairford. Most village church stained glass is depressingly gaudy and tasteless.

But first, it was the flowers that I saw, the wedding flowers, on every window ledge, on the steps, beside the altar and the font. The florists had not been allowed to do their worst either; these were country flowers for a country wedding, meadow and hedgerow and cottage garden flowers, with huge sprays of new beech leaves and great stems of creamy cow parsley, mixed with white daisies and lilac, arranged in good shapes in plain vases. I stood and looked at them and, as I stood, it seemed that the church was still quietly charged with all the emotion, the happiness and gravity, love and laughter and tearfulness, of that day's wedding, and somehow the music and the familiar, beautiful, solemn words still hung on the air. Who could not be blessed with a golden future, who could fail to go out into long life and married joy from such a church on such a day? So I sentimentally thought.

There are a lot of good things in Oddington church, and none of the horrors that so often blight the interiors of these medieval buildings. Principally, and most dramatically, there is the fourteenth-century painting on the north wall of the nave, a Doom, or Last Judgment. It is most realistic, gruesome in detail, with weird monsters and terrible torments depicted and a devil blowing up the fires of hell with bellows, while on the other side, the virtuous climb up to the Heavenly City, escorted by angels.

I am a great collector of Lion and Unicorn boards in churches, and Oddington has two, one over the chancel arch, and a splendid one, painted in rich dark colours on wood, at the back. And I always poke about among the pews in search of nice kneelers. Oddington's kneelers are *very* nice, and the best one has a Noah's Ark, with everything, as it should be, two by two.

I came outside again. The children were sitting on a gravestone beneath the down-spreading branches of a beech tree. I walked all the way round the church until I came back to the east end. There, on the wall, is a memorial tablet, dating from the seventeenth century, to many dead young children of one family, a moving thing, all sorrowing angels and visible sentiment. And on the grassy mound beside the wall, above the lane, is another memorial, less ostentatious, but much more useful, a wooden bench, set there in tribute to 'Samuel

and Ann Harrison'. And who would not remember them with gratitude, in such a spot, for there you face the tree-lined lane that curves away below and, through a gap in the trees, you look over a fold of perfect countryside, a sloping cornfield fringed by hedgerows.

I sat in the last of the sun. No one else had come here, there was no noise, but the trees whispered, the birds sang on and on, and behind me, the children's voices rose in laughter. And I thought nothing but good of St Nicholas, Oddington.

I said that in the morning we had left Oddington to its wedding and gone to market, to one of my favourite small market towns, in a region rich with them – Chipping Norton. And there isn't any doubt that it *is* a market town, not only because it looks like one, with its central square set on market days with stalls, but because its very name makes the statement – 'Chipping' comes from cheapen, the old word for a market. Locally, however, it is always known as Chippy.

But a few miles before you get to Chippy, on the main A.436 that leads from Stow-on-the-Wold, you will see a sign. Familiar perhaps. Adlestrop. Adlestrop? I feel a stir of affection when I read or hear the name, as if it were that of an old friend and it brings with it a whole train of associations in its wake, echoes of English poets and poetry and of nostalgia for the peace of remote rural villages half a century ago. One of the finest twentieth-century English poets and celebrants of the countryside, Edward Thomas, is best known for this one poem – Adlestrop.

Yes. I remember Adlestrop –
The name, because one afternoon
Of heat the express-train drew up there
Unwontedly. It was late June.

The steam hissed. Someone cleared his throat.
No one left and no one came
On the bare platform. What I saw
Was Adlestrop – only the name

And willows, willow-herb, and grass,
And meadowsweet, and haycocks dry,
No whit less still and lonely fair
Than the high cloudlets in the sky.

And for that minute a blackbird sang
Close by, and round him, mistier,
Farther and farther, all the birds
Of Oxfordshire and Gloucestershire.

I learned it when I was at school and I still know it by heart and when I pass the signpost pointing to Adlestrop, the opening stanzas begin to wind through my head. I am told that when they closed Adlestrop Station, they took down the sign Edward Thomas saw and put it up in the bus shelter, but I have never actually seen it because I have never been to Adlestrop and I don't want to go. The magic of the name and the beauty of the poem might be spoiled. I like to think that Adlestrop isn't a *real* place at all. So the signpost off the road points in a direction I shall never take.

On instead to Chippy and the best approach is on the A.44 from Moreton-in-Marsh to the north-west, down hill, with fields on either side and then, the sight of the town spread out on the hill ahead – for Chipping Norton stands high, high enough to catch the worst of the weather every winter and often to be cut off for days on end by the heavy snow blown up towards it.

As you approach the outskirts, before you climb the last steep hill that will bring you right into the market place, look right – not that you can avoid doing so; your eye is drawn to an astonishing sight. Anyone who enjoys the more eccentric buildings of England will feel gleeful indeed when confronting the Victorian Bliss Valley Tweed Mill. It looks like anything but a factory – a sort of cross between an extravagant stately home and a folly, with a great cupola out of which the huge chimney rises like a beacon. Some people think it is a monstrosity; more, including me, think it is wonderful, breathtaking in its position, peculiar, dramatic, amusing. Its lines are pleasing, it doesn't at all spoil the countryside, for all its incongruity, and it brings an unmistakable touch of Betjeman to the Oxfordshire Cotswolds.

Before you get right into the heart of Chipping Norton, stop, if you can possibly find one of the few parking spaces on the hill itself, and go across the road to walk under an archway and down the narrow lane that leads to the almshouses and then to the church dedicated to St Mary. It is a very fine, big church with the most wonderful soaring nave, with pillars that seem so elegant and graceful they are almost too fine for this workaday market town but ought to belong to one of the churches or chapels in the City of Oxford itself. I love this corner of Chippy, it is secluded and yet airy on top of the hill and if you have children, you can take them out of the church into the recreation ground where the swings and slides and roundabouts are set on as open and breezy and green a spot as you could wish for. Indeed, an unexpected aspect of visiting Cotswold towns and villages with small people has been the discovery of so many pretty country playgrounds where they can swing and slide and run about in the midst of verdant surroundings.

Chipping Norton has been a place to which we have made family expeditions for years. We know it for

The Wednesday market in Chipping Norton, popular with both locals and visitors

The Rollright Stones: The King's Men stone circle

shopping and having lunches out and teatime treats, and for one of those old-fashioned sweet shops where things are still in big jars not packets, and you find sweets like Satin Cushions and Sherbet Pips and Aniseed Balls which you didn't think they made any more. We feel at home in the place and I don't see how you could not. It is friendly, small, compact and busy, the shopping centre for a lot of villages around.

And look up, above the glinting steel roofs of the parked cars, above the horrible shop fascias and see just how many extraordinarily handsome houses, mainly eighteenth century, Chipping Norton market place boasts of. That's always another slightly surprising thing about the Cotswolds: you expect the honey-coloured cottages and the golden-stone manor houses but not the plain, austere, elegant Georgian town houses of Cirencester and Fairford, Painswick and Chipping Norton.

I have complained about the shop signs and fascias. I complain about them in every town and village I ever visit. You would never believe that planning permission had to be granted for them and that it is supposedly particularly strict in conservation areas and for listed buildings. There are the usual excrescences in Chipping Norton but some notable exceptions too – all the banks have taken care to keep their façades looking exactly right and so have most of the antique shops and a few others owned individually. As always, it is the chain and group stores which are mostly to blame. And if only here, as everywhere, I could banish the motor car to some deep underground pit. What Cotswold market squares and streets looked like less than one hundred years ago doesn't only have to be imagined, you can see it from old photographs and picture postcards.

From Chipping Norton, the last outpost of the Cotswolds on this side of Oxfordshire, we generally return home. But occasionally we make a detour, going north for a few miles on the country road through Over Norton that leads up towards the Rollrights – not so much to visit the Rollright villages, pleasant though they are, but to go to the Rollright Stones. The ghosts of pre-history haunt the whole Cotswold region but nowhere do they cry so loudly on the whistling wind as in that bleak eerie field around which stand the odd, rounded Rollright Stones in their circle. A 'witchy' place, my eldest daughter calls it and so it is, if you go alone on a winter's afternoon when the skies are gathering and dark comes early. I am not sure why. So often such places give me a sense of nothing at all very much, but standing in the middle of the Rollrights, wondering whether it might really be true that they are uncountable, I always feel a chill in my bones and want to glance uneasily over my shoulder. But we go back to them still, drawn by their strangeness and age and the puzzlement of it all – *what* are they, who set them here, exactly when, and above all why, why?

I said that I don't like main roads but when we leave the Rollrights, I am actually rather relieved to be on one, among other cars and other people making ordinary journeys, needing to be reassured that I am safely in the twentieth century and on the way back home.

The Whispering Knights: this is thought to be the remains of a burial chamber

Uplands and Wetlands

(Above) *The Windrush Valley near Burford;*
(right) *the western scarp of the Cotswolds looking south from Haresfield Beacon*

3. Chipping Campden

Cornwell – Chastleton – Moreton-in-Marsh – Batsford Arboretum – Bourton-on-the-Hill – Blockley – Chipping Campden

Certain places suit certain seasons best. I'm not sure why that should be – it has to do with small, subtle things like the lie of the land, the particular trees, presence or absence of hedgerows, the mood rather than the architecture of a house or a group of cottages. In the Cotswolds, places and how you feel about them can change quite dramatically according to the time of year, the weather, the quality of the light. People have told me of a gloriously romantic and secluded spot; perhaps they have only seen it on perfect, brilliant, cloudless days of June when the air is bright with butterflies, the countryside drowsy with the drone of bees, and all looks golden and enticing, for when I have been there, I have found it gloomy and oppressive. But not everyone allows their judgment to be so affected by a passing cloud, momentary darkness and a wind that blows suddenly cold; they probably look at the Cotswolds with a clearer, steadier eye.

There is one journey that I have made at every time of year and in all sorts of weather, and it passes through places which I love, and respond to with happiness no matter when I see them. Their moods are changeable, they can look very different according to the day but I never tire of them, am always ready to go back.

But, if I can choose a season, autumn is best of all. Wait for one of those perfect days at the end of September which begin with a cold dawn and a clammy, eerie early mist which lies like a vapour very low over the fields, shifting, swirling, thinning and then suddenly clotting together again. You cannot see further than the first few yards into the field beyond the five-barred gate.

Then something happens, some change in temperature, or shift of the wind, invisible, unguessable, but it causes the mist to disperse, evaporate, disintegrate. One moment it is all around you, you can smell it, touch it, taste its strange rusty coldness if you open your mouth, it leaves little beads of moisture clinging to your sleeve; the next, it is not there, the sun is up and shafting through, and the hedgerows, the bars of every gate, the struts of every fence, are shimmering with iridescent jewels of moisture and laced over with a delicate tracery of spiders' webs. And deep in the grass, the creamy white mounds of mushrooms and puffballs, and the glory of a million dandelion clocks.

Take to the road now, as quickly as you can, and especially if it is Sunday, it will be quiet.

From where I live, it is west and then north until the Oxford to Stratford road, and on through the village of Enstone that runs with the steep line of the hill, down and then up again. A mile or so out of Enstone, there is a sign to the left. Lidstone. From

(Opposite) *The Lime Avenue, Batsford Park*

here, take a narrow road that rises through quiet farmland, skirting south of Chipping Norton. Soon you begin to follow signs that read Cornwell. From up here, you can see half of Oxfordshire ahead, the slopes rising up in a ridge above the line of the river Evenlode, wooded here and there, and chequered like patchwork, some fields already ploughed to red-brown earth again, others striped and charred after stubble-burning, a few still golden with corn. There are plenty of hedge-rows, too, rich-ripe with berries, elder, sloe, hawthorn. Every year, there seem to be more berries than ever before, and every year someone says it will be a hard winter, and every year it either is, or is not, but the berries never seem to fail or diminish.

Anywhere along here, you can stop and find black-berries, and eat them straight off the bush, fresh and sharp enough to pucker up the inside of your mouth, but oddly sweet at the same time, and wonderfully purple-staining of fingers. This is one of my favourite roads in the whole of the Cotswolds, though it is not perhaps very 'Cotswold' at all. The countryside is on the very edge, one way Oxfordshire, but when you reach the hamlet of Cornwell that lies in a dip off the narrow road, then you know for certain you are in the Cotswolds.

It was very late one autumn Sunday when I first came upon Cornwell; after being out to lunch with friends, we had taken a back road we didn't know, hoping to avoid the busy, main A.44.

I remember saying, 'Cornwell with an "e" – I wonder what that is.' And then we came upon it.

You have to leave the car on the road, and walk down the little lane leading in amongst the cottages – and entering, it is almost like going into a miniature village, everything seems on a smaller scale. I don't quite know *why* I get that impression here but I always do.

Cornwell is all of a piece, very compact, an estate village all belonging to the big house. I suppose some will find it altogether *too* neat, with not a blade of grass

out of place, but when you walk about it, it is very quiet, very well kept, and it feels entirely welcoming and friendly.

That first day, we were wanting to get home, uncertain of the way, but as we drove off again, I chanced to look left through an elaborate gate set between stone pillars. And saw one of those perfect houses that seem to happen in this part of England as nowhere else, a vision of it glimpsed beyond the gateway, at the end of a grassy drive. I braked hard, and reversed. Could I believe my eyes?

I have stopped here many, many times since that day, stood for a few moments at those gates, and looked down in quiet pleasure at the beautiful stone manor, framed by the pillars of the gateway and a fringe of tree branches. It stands, cool and grey and settled within itself on the other side of a flat Italianate lily pond, the sort of house you read about in stories, slightly mysterious but not forbidding, entirely private but seeming, by the very self-consciousness of its half-hidden, yet just-visible position, to beckon you to want to be admired.

When later I consulted Pevsner's *Buildings of England*, it told me that 'the village west of the house has been almost entirely rebuilt in a stagey manner by Clough Williams Ellis'. Well, well. I went to look again at Cornwell, wondering if this knowledge that it is, after all, a slightly artificial place, makes any difference to my enjoyment of it. And decided that it does not, for Cornwell still feels real, is lived in, it is not a film-set of a place like Castle Combe or Laycock, if only because it is simply a bit more obscure, less visited by crowds of sightseers. Cornwell keeps its slight air of privacy. And, with the passing of time, even Ellis's work has mellowed and blended with the older remains of the village.

And if that is true of lovely, elegant Cornwell, lying

Cornwell Manor

peaceful in the September sun, how much more so of the house you come to after that.

Chastleton is quite extraordinary. As I write, it still exists as it has done for almost three hundred and ninety years, its exterior and interior scarcely altered. It seems to lie in a sort of time-warp, to belong entirely to the past, to an age long dead. It reminds me, just a little, of Miss Havisham's house in which all the clocks stood still, and the wedding cake and the bridal veil and all the hangings and draperies and furnishings were held together by nothing more than cobwebs and dust. Go into Chastleton and blow hard – and might it not simply disintegrate to a handful of dust?

Chastleton itself is a small village set among quiet fields, a few miles from the market town of Moreton-in-Marsh. It is one of the drowsiest places I have ever been to, a village where nothing ever seems to be disturbed, nothing changes, nothing happens. The countryside that spreads out around it is undulating, gentle, sheltered, with grazing fields, hay meadows, sloping pasture and well-kept parkland rich in mature trees.

As you enter it from the direction of Cornwell, you see, in the middle of an uphill sloping field, an eighteenth-century stone dovecote, designed like a

Chastleton House

small version of one of the Cotswold market halls, with arches and a mossy tiled roof (as the ones at Chipping Campden and Minchinhampton). Set there among sheep and great, graceful trees, it is surprising but utterly right, it draws the eye to itself and fits harmoniously into the landscape.

Park under the trees in a clearing beside the little church of St Mary. The paling bends round with the sharp curve of the lane, and there, beside the church, at the end of a gravelled drive, is Chastleton House, a completely unaltered Jacobean house.

It has had a chequered history. It was begun by one of the numerous wool merchants wanting to establish his family as landed gentry, but by the time it was complete, the wool-based economy had begun to collapse, and the family bought no more land and could barely support the house. And so it has been down the centuries, neglected, allowed to deteriorate, restored a little, always costing more to keep in good repair than could be afforded..

As I write, it is still in private hands, open to the public on summer weekend afternoons, still just poised on the brink of dilapidation and collapse, and yet a magnificent survival. It has panelling, moulding, plaster-work and carving intact since the house was begun in 1603. It has furnishings, tapestries, hangings, threadbare but original. It has holes in the oak floor boards, breaks and cracks in the ornate ceilings, an air of desperation as though the forces of darkness were just – just – held at bay. It smells of cats and gas and age; there are trays of dusty cacti in pots on the cobwebbed window ledges, a collection of priceless porcelain, some very good and a lot of very bad pictures, a chained Bible and, above all, a quite magnificent gallery, worth coming a thousand miles to see.

In the gardens, topiary-work, archways with climbing roses – and the wilderness beyond, encroaching ever nearer.

I have seen Chastleton at dusk when the clouds raced, on late autumn afternoons when the shadows began to lengthen across the grass and the air struck suddenly damp and chill. I have seen it rising faint and grey, like a Scottish castle, behind its closed gates in the winter snow. It looks as if it had been painted by John Piper at his most theatrical, a back-drop to some Jacobean opera. It broods, and time must surely be running out for it to continue to survive like this.

I have no doubt that all manner of respectable and worthy bodies are poised in the wings, waiting for Chastleton. That one day, an army of restorers and conservationists and cleaners will descend upon it, that inside there will be roped-off areas and printed signs about not touching, and the whole will smell of lavender polish and be a museum, not a home. I shall hate it then. I like Chastleton now, hanging on, belonging to real people, the bills piling up, the roof beginning to leak, the corridors still haunted by friendly ghosts, and all its history and romance still, just, clinging to it.

Autumn is the time of year for fairs and horticultural shows, and you may catch either in this part of the Cotswolds. If there is a fair, the centre of any one of

Moreton-in-Marsh, and its Market Hall

half a dozen market towns will be closed off by barriers, and given over to dodgem cars and carousels, to stalls and booths and caravans, coconut shies and fortune tellers, while the air will be full of the burnt-sugar smell of candy floss and the frying of a hundred burgers. I suppose you either love them or hate them. Either way, they are fleeting enough, crowding the square today and full of flashing, whirring lights and gaudy music tonight, and gone, quite gone, in the morning.

A Cotswold fair, at night

But surely no one in the world on a fine September day could do anything but love the annual show and gymkhana, in town and village all over the Cotswolds. The gathering of so many proud horses and ponies-and-traps to compete for all those rosettes, the tents full of such magnificent produce displays – onions the size of footballs, beans as straight as rulers and a myriad jars of glowing preserves. It is all as good, as bustling, as local as market day. After it, the nights begin to draw more quickly in. The year is slipping downhill, and all over the Cotswold countryside, the air is pungent with the smoke of bonfires.

The market town of Moreton-in-Marsh always seems

to be busy. Leave your car and walk all the way up to the top of the main street, and all the way down again on the other side. It's the best way to see the houses which are all pleasing, a companionable assortment of seventeenth- and eighteenth-century stone buildings, mainly quite low and with some lovely façades, doors, windows, roofs.

Moreton is not entirely sure whether to be a tourist town of the Cotswolds or not. It has kept a foot in the door; there is a decent selection of tea rooms and restaurants and several hotels, more than a few antique shops, a nod in the direction of gifts and souvenirs – you can buy guide books and postcards and little china thimbles saying 'A present from the Cotswolds'. But really, I don't think Moreton-in-Marsh has its heart in tourism, it is too much of a real place, a centre, like Chipping Norton, for the villages and outlying farms around. You can buy a good yard-brush, a fresh chicken, a pair of wellington boots or a television set here as easily as an antique oak settle or a piece of Wedgwood giftware. The shops are all small and generally full, the pavements narrow and generally crowded and, inevitably, the town has a serious traffic problem. The main road flows directly through, cutting the two sides of the long street in half, dangerous and difficult to cross as heavy lorries, farm traffic, coaches and a large volume of cars pour past. Moreton-in-Marsh, like so many Cotswolds towns, desperately needs a bypass.

It is a growing town too, spreading out with new housing, and becoming popular among 'incomers', for there is a train from here to Paddington, and plenty of people are brave, or desperate, enough to commute to work in London.

I have grown rather fond of Moreton over the years, though when I took a friend there recently, she could not see the charm of it at all. I suppose it marks a stage on the road towards all manner of places which I especially like. Certainly, Moreton-in-Marsh is a meeting place of roads, from Stow, from Broadway, from Chipping Norton and Chipping Campden – you pass through it en route to everywhere, which is its principal problem.

Autumn is the time for trees, for red and gold, russet and flame, and the first falling of leaves, the very last sight of a stray swallow. September and October, my favourite months of the year, heavy with scents and rich with colours, sweet with nostalgia. Now is the best time of all to go on from the bustle of Moreton to the arboretum, where the trees will take your breath away, showy and proud in the last of their glory.

Batsford Arboretum lies just outside the town to the right of the A.44 that leads up to Bourton-on-the-Hill and Broadway. It occupies a south-eastern facing slope that looks towards Moreton, and so over the whole Evenlode valley, and here and there they have placed benches very carefully so that you can sit and see below, through a gap in the trees, the gentle countryside and the roofs of the little town.

Bourton-on-the-Hill looking towards Moreton-in-Marsh;
(opposite) *Batsford Arboretum*

Here is a peaceful, cool, calming place to walk. If you are a serious tree-fancier, you can discover from a well-laid-out plan in the guide book that this is one of the most comprehensive collections of trees in the country. If you are not, you can simply enjoy the curious leaf-mould and tree-bark smell, and the rays of sunlight striking through like the spokes of a shining, outspread fan; feel the spongy, damp grass and pine-needle carpet beneath your feet, listen to the cheeping

of all the pheasants which are bred here and wander freely, tamely about. I know of few places which have such a soothing, tranquil atmosphere as Batsford Arboretum. Trees grow slowly, silently, and yet you can stand in the midst of them and almost feel them doing it, and feel, too, the great strength of them, and the force of the life that courses upwards through their great trunks and out to the tips of all the branches.

Return to the A.44 which begins to climb towards the pretty picture-book village of Bourton-on-the Hill. The cottages have the most cottagey gardens hereabouts, but the village is wrecked by having the traffic running right through it, slow and noisy going up the

One of the many fine kitchen gardens in the Cotswolds

steep hill, dangerously fast, ignoring all the speed limit signs, coming down.

I have an old postcard of Bourton-on-the-Hill with a flock of sheep being driven through the main street on a summer's evening. It must have been lovely then.

Most people drive through the village with scarcely a glance to either side. It pays to go slowly, to find a parking spot off the main road, and to go for a walk among the cottages, down the lanes leading away from the hill, and to stand looking over the downs that run away towards the valley. In September, the gardens are purple with Michaelmas daisies; the last of the hollyhocks, all blowsy petals and washed-out colours, stand tall beside the sunflowers against grey stone walls; the wigwams of beans are like green and scarlet tents, the dahlias glow, a late rose in its final flush flowers around a door.

Just outside Bourton-on-the-Hill, there is a road off to the right. Take it. It leads to Blockley, one of the best of all Cotswold villages. Blockley that begins low down and climbs up the steep hill to end standing proud and high, overlooking miles of the surrounding counties, Blockley which has old silk mills and rows of weavers' cottages, and villas with wrought-iron porches, and a playground where children can swing up high and see for mile after mile, feel as if they were on top of the world. Blockley has a very strongly unified local population, and a lot of weekenders from London and, whenever I have been there, summer or winter, apparently no tourists at all.

Because of its high situation and its unusual architecture, Blockley has a very different feel from the Cotswold villages and market towns that surround it, yet nothing seems out of place. Up at the top of the village, the wind blows, and wherever you walk there

(Above) *A terrace of houses in Blockley;* (below) *the view from the recreation ground*

are marvellous vistas of the valley below. Down the slopes, where the brook winds, all is sheltered and snug, the air feels warmer.

The church is a surprise, too – very spacious and light, a little formal, a little cold, with a great many monuments. It is a self-important sort of church, lying on the slope; a church that belongs, in size and feel, to the large and prosperous industrial village that Blockley once was.

Blockley is a place I can never just drive through. I always want to stop there – to walk on the recreation ground that looks down onto the perfect sward of the bowling green, to climb up and down the steep lanes between cottages, to stand beside the murmuring brook, to sit on a summer's day at a table outside the pub, watching the village go about its business and admiring the design and presentation of the pretty Regency cottages nearby. Blockley has given me, over the years, a lot of quiet pleasure.

And so, towards the very end of a golden afternoon, the road leads on, across the roof of the north Cotswolds. Here you can feel the air rush towards you from far, far away, the sky is very close. At the highest point in the road, you stand and look down, and there is that most wonderful, breathtaking of Cotswold sights – the butter-and-honey-coloured houses of Chipping Campden, clustered together and resting, like a quilt on a bed, in the plain below. The tower – the most handsome in the whole region – has gilded weather vanes upon each of its pinnacles, flying like angels in the late light of the sun.

I almost prefer to stay at a distance, looking down like this on Campden, than dropping into it. I can think of few places which blend so perfectly, so exactly, into their surroundings. Plenty of towns and villages in the Cotswolds lie in the fold of a hill, or spread out on the flat with slopes rising all around; it is a familiar

Chipping Campden church on a hazy summer afternoon

Chipping Campden. (Opposite) *The church of St James.* (Above) *Distant view of the church in the evening light and* (below) *the high street at the end of the day*

feature as you travel the whole region, but nowhere does it quite so well as Campden.

But it is a good place to be in, too, a place I have known and loved for years, and written about before. I still think the curve of the High Street the best in the Cotswolds, the church and its very large churchyard the finest of all the great wool churches, the open-ness and green-ness on Campden's doorstep so refreshing. One of the best of pleasures is to walk up the slope past the almshouses, and stand at the gate leading to the church – turn, and look back. The green hills rise up all around, over the rooftops. The much-photographed row of almshouses never fails to impress because of the grace of its proportions, the lovely soft colour of the stone, the way the road curves and rises.

Campden always feels like a place to come home to at the end of the day, a secure, warm sort of town, and always quiet once the shops have closed and the home-coming traffic has gone.

Beyond it, we are out of the Cotswolds and away into Warwickshire and the Shakespeare country in one direction, in another to the lush, flat, fertile Vale of Evesham that borders the Cotswold ridge.

Once the sun has set, the autumn mist begins to creep back, the chill and the damp to settle in the bottom of hedgerows and over the quiet fields. There may be a first touch of frost, and the smell of it will linger on into the grey dawn, blackening flowers, pinching, withering. The seasons always feel very close to you in the Cotswolds, however sheltered you are in the heart of a village or town. Country is just beyond the door, over the stone wall, at the end of the lane, foxes will creep into back gardens and the owls will cry clear in the night.

Perhaps that is why I love it so much. And in autumn, with the snows and winds of winter so very near, I love this corner of the Cotswolds best of all.

The almshouses at Chipping Campden

4. Burford

'We started on a ten-mile jog along the Merlinford road, a sort of hog's back, more cruelly exposed than any road I have ever known, without a scrap of shelter or windscreen.'

The passage comes from Nancy Mitford's autobiographical novel, in part about the years of her Cotswold childhood, *The Pursuit of Love* – and it describes how the young Fanny is being led on her pony, at the end of an exhilarating day's hunting, through wind and driving rain along the road to home. The book is magical, one of the favourite books of my lifetime, and the road is one I know well and often travel on, the A.40 which runs along the top of the valley through which the main section of the River Windrush flows. It is indeed a hog's back of a road, and there is still no shelter as the winds sweep across, and though nowadays most people travel on it by car, there are still riders and walkers who will appreciate young Fanny's discomfort.

It is along this road that one realises that Cotswold country has begun, for suddenly the fields are crossed and bounded by those beautiful, typical dry-stone walls, yards of them, the grey-green-buff patterns within them as good-looking, practical and ancient a use of Cotswold stone as all the walls of manor houses and tithe barns, churches and cottages.

A little further on in the chapter, Fanny is at last

leaving the high road, and dropping down to the family home which lies in the valley below. Following her, as I have so often done, brings me to the village of Swinbrook, the Mitford village, in which Nancy's family lived, and in whose lovely churchyard both she and her sister Unity are now buried. The church stands proud on a high bank looking down over the pretty village, with its stream running through and its wide ford.

St Mary's is a beautiful building outside and even better within. My very favourite sort of church, in fact, with clear glass in the East window through which the pale Cotswold light comes streaming, and beyond which you glimpse sky and open fields and hills, so that the countryside is part of and almost *inside* the church, yet separated from it.

One of the delightful curiosities is the monuments to the local family, the Fettiplaces, whose aloof, stone

(Opposite) Burford seen across the Windrush Valley; (right) St Mary, Swinbrook

effigies lie stacked above one another, as though on shelves. They make me smile. There ought always to be something inside a church that has that effect, but there rarely is.

Only a mile beyond Swinbrook lies another special place, a tiny church set by itself in the middle of flat marshy fields, close to the river – it is almost as though it has been washed up there. St Oswald's Widford has the same light airiness of Swinbrook church, but while that is lofty and formally impressive, St Oswald's is intimate, quiet. It reminds me of the rather similar small church across the road from Hailes Abbey; stand inside and you feel the same way as if you are within an open barn or a spacious stone-flagged farmhouse, not a dark musty church. There are fragments of Roman flooring and some wall-paintings here, and high-backed pews with doors to them. When I last went, the fields from Swinbrook were boggy, the river flowing over its banks all around; even the daylight itself seemed watery. But the weak March sun shone in through the windows of the small church and made the dust dance, and the whole effect was as though one was in not a solid building but rather an ark upon the waters.

From Swinbrook and Widford, peaceful in their lush and sodden pastures, it is only a little way on to the first of the Cotswold market towns on this eastern edge of the Cotswolds. If you take that high road again and approach it from the top, you see Burford's wide and steep main street unwind like braid down the hill to the Windrush. Go very early in the morning, for even

in the depths of winter Burford is busy and besieged by visitors, and it suffers as badly as any of its fellow market towns from heavy traffic. It is naturally by-passed by the Oxford to Cheltenham road running across the top, but is still on the through-route from Lechlade to Stow-on-the-Wold. Much used by heavy lorries, as well as by all the tourist and domestic traffic, Burford, like everywhere else, needs a complete by-pass – but the county plan has deemed that it comes well down on the list. Residents and visitors will go on suffering.

There are some quiet corners in Burford, but none of them as they were when I spent three weeks there in October twenty years ago. I wanted to get away from the telephone and routine domestic distractions, to finish a novel in peace. Instead of taking a cottage in the depths of the country, or a house overlooking the North Sea – two other hideouts I regularly made for – I stayed in a hotel in Burford, working in a small room under the eaves and overlooking a cobbled courtyard. I don't suppose I could be so undisturbed and peaceful there now – and the hotel would prove inordinately expensive. I couldn't go for walks down the side streets and lanes of the town, or even in the main high street once the shops had closed, and see so few people.

My memories of Burford, like all such memories, are blurred and softened and made golden by time. I remember my weeks there fondly and, indeed, in spite of the crowds and the cars and the usual proliferation of gift shops, I am still very fond of it. Fond of the view down the hill. Fond of standing by the bridge which crosses the river and looking up to see the houses climb like packs of cards pulled outwards on either side of the road as it rises. Fond of Sheep Street, with its ivy-clad, grey stone hotels and its trees; and the offices of that wonderfully old-fashioned magazine

Fronts of some Burford shops . . .

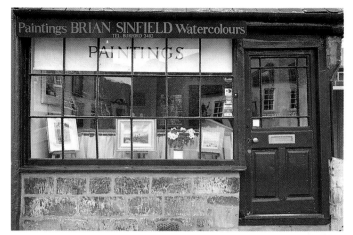

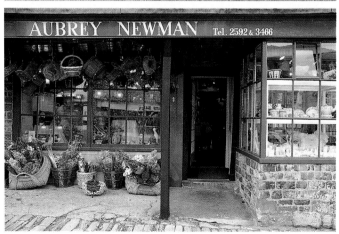

The Countryman. Fond of the fine church, with its spire, 'slender as a wand', and the close of almshouses, and the views of the water meadows and the Windrush with its fishermen glimpsed here and there. Fond of individual shops, too: the one with the antique clocks and the one which sells wood-burning stoves and stone garden ornaments, Grecian ladies and swagged urns and sundials, and the shop with some of the best home-made cakes in the Cotswolds, whose smell wafts tantalisingly into your nostrils half way up the high street.

Shops are very important in the Cotswold region – and they are mainly small and privately owned. Plenty of village shops still exist, though a good many more have gone out of business in recent years. But enter any one of them, and the general atmosphere has not changed, though there may be self-service and a stack of supermarket style wire baskets, however cramped the space.

There will often be a minute post office section at the back, and the shop may double as a newsagent, tobacconist and sweetie shop, too. Otherwise, there will be groceries and greengroceries cheek by jowl with greeting cards and garden implements, bubble bath and bread, a few toys and children's plimsolls. The smell of the village shop is as distinctive as that of the church and, above all, they are social centres where everyone still knows the shopkeeper and there are notices for village activities and requirements on the door. I have bought many a packet of mints and cans of soft drink, ice cream or pint of milk in them, and everywhere I have been greeted cheerfully and in friendliness.

In the market towns, shops matter not only for the obvious reasons but because they form the focus of visits and the reason for a journey: they, too, are social centres, particularly for the elderly and the solitary.

. . . the high street is full of colour and variety

They provide jobs in areas where, apart from those in farming and tourism, there may be few, and their appearance is important because, on going into a town, down a main thoroughfare or into a square, shops are what are seen; they dominate, when grouped together, and they alter, enhance or dictate – or, sadly, all too often spoil – the whole architectural look and feel of a town.

Some remain places to which local people and those from the surrounding countryside come to do their daily or weekly household shopping, and they make few concessions to tourism. There may be an antique shop here and there, the post office may sell maps, guide-books and a few souvenirs but, in general, they are mainly real shops selling useful and necessary items, the butchers, and bakers, and candlestick makers of the Cotswolds.

Other towns have given themselves over to the demands – or rather what it is supposed are the demands – of visitors. In these, it is very hard to find the chemist, the hardware store or the supermarket: if they exist at all, they are hidden away in side streets, or among new houses on roads leading out of the town – where the rates are always cheaper. The main streets are filled with shops selling Scottish woollens, Waterford crystal and Royal Worcester china, expensive teddy bears wearing Union Jacks, and all manner of elaborately packaged confectionery and toiletries. Souvenirs and gifts have gone up-market in certain Cotswold towns, though in Bourton-on-the-Water and Moreton-in-Marsh you can still find mugs and ashtrays with 'a present from . . .'.

Burford is gradually becoming more and more a tourist town in shopping terms. The favourite activity of visitors seems to be strolling up one side of the Cotswold shopping street, and down the other, browsing and buying so, not surprisingly, shopkeepers who cater for them have proliferated.

I would not wish to live there, nor even to stay for very long again, though perhaps in mid-week January I might still find a peaceful corner of a quiet hotel in which to work. And, like any other tourist town, Burford does have a private life; community spirit is very strong here, and local pride, too. The business of Cotswold towns may often be seasonal, but they are not by any means dead places for the rest of the time. Church activities, social clubs, women's institutes, drama groups, local history societies, evening classes, charity bazaars and coffee mornings, whist drives and bridge evenings, youth clubs and tennis and cricket and bowls – all thrive. The spirit of the Cotswolds is to be found, as much as anywhere, on the notice boards announcing parish events.

I've made as many journeys into the Cotswolds in winter as in spring and summer and, like the young Fanny in Nancy Mitford's novel, have found the winds blowing cold, cold indeed across those open fields; have seen the sheep huddled together for warmth, and watched my breath smoke up into the chill air of the empty churches. On one of the coldest days at the end of January, I came to Little Barrington, a few minutes out of Burford, going west. There was a little shelter from the wind here, and the sky was an achingly bright blue; the sun shone, though there was no warmth in it. And everywhere in the Cotswolds that day there were snowdrops – in churchyards and rectory gardens, in manor house gardens and cottage gardens, under trees, in ditches, up banks, singly, in clumps and clusters, and spreading out into pools of white.

Little Barrington is a village of ancient, silent stone houses, set all around a sort of scrubby green which dips down like a bowl at the centre to a stream, and rises around in bumps and hollows. This is the site of a former quarry; from here, the Barrington stone once came. Now the snowdrops are thick in the deep tussocky grass, and the stream, when I bent to put my hand in its water, was like an ice floe. A tethered goat stood looking melancholy at the grass, and a woman wrapped up in layers of coat and scarf sat painting at

an easel. Otherwise, Little Barrington was empty and silent. And had a strange ghostly air which I had been aware of when I had come before: strange because not unfriendly, not unpleasant – but definite, as though some rather contented people who once lived and worked in this tiny village had left something of themselves behind.

Great Barrington, a much larger village on the other side of the Windrush, has a haunted air of a very different kind, melancholy, dispirited. It has been neglected for many years, a lot of the cottages have been allowed to fall into a sad state of disrepair or even complete dereliction.

I walked slowly up the street. Here a roof had fallen

in, there a window was boarded up, a flight of stone steps cracked and broken, a door missing, even a completely roofless shell of a stone building. But then, in other parts of the village, there were men at work, repairing, even reconstructing, so I stopped to talk to one of them who was very carefully restoring a moulded drip-course around the top of a window. I was told that there was a new landlord – for Great Barrington is an estate village – who was doing everything he could, as fast as he could, to resurrect the village which had been neglected for so many years.

I was able to leave the village with a gladdened heart; Great Barrington had obviously been a beautiful village – and will be again.

From Great Barrington, retrace your steps a little, passing Barrington Park, a Palladian mansion set among wide, tree-filled acres. Take the road that runs back up the valley of the river Windrush which has been winding its way through lush meadows. Go through the village of Windrush itself – a nice blend of the old, with some mainly good new. Stop to visit St Peter's church with its wonderful south door, and then on to a much more remarkable place.

Sherborne is a planned village. It has the most lovely parkland set on either side of Sherborne Brook

Gravestones in the churchyard at Sherborne

(a tributary of the Windrush) with a weir, a waterfall, meadows, sloping fields set about with the best of trees, and Sherborne House (now a school) with the church beside it. But it is the layout of its estate cottages which lends Sherborne its very particular charm. There are eleven small rows of them, mainly built alongside the road but, in one or two cases, set at right angles. They are, I suppose, the private, rural equivalent of council houses, but how much better designed and built, how much more in keeping with the rest of the landscape and architecture of the village than most modern country council houses which are usually such awful prefabricated or cement-faced blots on the landscape. The Sherborne cottages are early Victorian, stone-built, neat, low, compact, with long front gardens and paths running up to them. One of them houses the village post office.

Sherborne is a long, long village, wending its way beside the brook for almost a mile. If you had a little boat, you could take to the water, and row gently down to where Sherborne Brook joins the Windrush, and then north against the flow, through nothing but open fields, between rushy banks, all the way to the small town of Bourton-on-the-Water. It would be a wonderful, leisurely, Ratty-and-Mole sort of adventure for a summer's afternoon, with picnics under willow trees, the most romantic way of seeing the Cotswold countryside.

If, more prosaically, you choose to go by road, the best route is back to Great Barrington, and so up, through Great and Little Rissington which stand high looking down on the Windrush valley.

And now, at Bourton-on-the-Water, you are in the centre of major tourist activity. From here, it is only a few miles to Stow-on-the-Wold, via Lower and Upper Slaughter, with the Swells – also Lower and Upper – nearby. It is to these places that all the coaches come,

Sherborne Brook

through them that the Americans pass on their Cotswold tours. The school parties and day trippers, the shoppers and picnickers all converge upon Bourton and Stow; both places have spread and have new housing developments in and around them. I find it impossible to judge them fairly, to know whether I find them attractive architecturally or not, for there is never a day now, winter or summer – and certainly never a weekend – when they are not crowded, and the consequent traffic jams are considerable and quite unbearable.

Bourton-on-the-Water is the most obviously attractive – a wide main square, with the River Windrush running through its gardens, and little bridges leading over. There are shady small streets off the square and a pleasant walk, following the water, down to the meadows near a trout hatchery. The bird gardens are pleasant with cockatoos flying free in the trees,

flamingoes with amazing pink legs on the lawn, and penguins diving for fish at feeding time. Children love it, and I much prefer a bird garden, even with cages, to a zoo in which large animals are confined. Further down the main street, on the opposite side of the road, is the model village which has the Lilliputian charm of all such places – I always wish I had been there as a child, when I was in proportion with the buildings; the amusement of the model village in which you find a model village, in which you find . . . is never failing. Children are fascinated by it.

As a day-out sort of place, in company with a great many other people, there is plenty to be said for Bourton-on-the-Water. There are plenty of pubs, cafés and restaurants, shops galore, nice benches on which to sit and watch the world go by, ducks to feed. I should like to have come to Bourton two hundred years ago, but it is easy to see the charm of the place since water running under bridges through the streets of any town or village always attracts.

A friend of mine calls it the Blackpool of the Cotswolds. I know what he means. And Blackpool has its place – I rather like it.

I don't much care for Stow-on-the-Wold though, and when I was last there, I walked around trying to understand what has made it such a honeypot for tourists. It has no obvious attraction; it is bleak, grey, plain and really rather ordinary, and getting into and out of it, from the busiest road junction in the region, is always a nightmare. I suppose the fact that it is on the junction of so many routes has made it a convenient stopping-off place, and so the tea shops and gift shops have grown up in response to the ever-increasing number of visitors.

The market square is large and the houses good, solid stone ones – but not by any means as good as those of Broadway. There aren't very many Cotswold places which seem to me nowadays to have no atmosphere at all, but Stow is certainly one.

The River Eye runs through (left) *Lower Slaughter and* (right) *Upper Slaughter*

(Opposite) *Stow-in-the-Wold from the top of the church tower, the Cotswold landscape beyond;* (above) *autumn morning on the River Eye*

Not far away from Stow, to the west, are those other well-known tourist spots, the Swells and the Slaughters (each has an Upper and a Lower). The Slaughters are the most often photographed, most driven through by the round-tour coaches. And yes, indeed, they are very charming. They are pretty and picturesque, and the stone houses are mellow, and the greensward very green, the trees hang low and leafy, the streams trickle lazily through. But there are many other villages I like better, and which have not been picked out as representative beauty spots.

However, there is a corner of this little area of the Cotswold countryside I would exchange for the whole of Stow, the Swells and the Slaughters put together. There is a very, very minor road, leading from Lower to Upper Swell. Half way along it, stop, and look right. The church tower and the roofs of Stow rise up out of the surrounding fields and above the line of the trees. It is not a spectacular view, merely harmonious, with the rise of the ground and the sweep of the fields, and the grace and shape of all the trees complementing one another, and the stone church for the eye to rest on at the climax of the view. Stand here, beside the hedge, and you will hear no traffic, probably see no other human beings.

Late on a summer's afternoon, when the air took on an indescribable soft golden clarity that bathed the undulating fields in a perfect light, I stood, simply looking and being, and the mysterious spirit of the Cotswolds was all around – but what it was, I could not have told.

5. Broadway

Broadway – Buckland – Stanton and Stanway – Hailes – Broadway Country Park – Snowshill – Guiting Power – Naunton

I've been to Broadway quite often in the course of the past fifteen years or so. Often, I've simply been driving through it, on my way to somewhere else, but occasionally I have taken a visiting friend and gone there for tea, or stopped to buy a present. And, on weekend or weekday, at any season of the year, it has always been busy. The surrounding countryside may be quiet, the tourists may apparently all have fled – but Broadway will be packed with coaches and cars.

The last time I went was on a Monday morning in July, and I arrived before nine o'clock because I had been thinking a lot about Broadway, wondering what exactly it was that made it such a honeypot, and I thought that if I could stroll about before the shops opened, and before the holidaymakers had finished breakfast, I might be able actually to see the town itself and reach some conclusions about it. I didn't expect silent streets and a complete absence of cars and people, but I was unprepared for what I did find.

As you drive in, from any direction, you see signs. 'Broadway needs a By-pass *now*'. It wasn't until I'd parked in the main street and begun to walk slowly up the hill that I fully appreciated how right they are. At that time, as at all times of day, the look of the long, wide, handsome street was spoiled by the ugly fringe of parked cars, but that is true now of almost every main street in every town and village in the Cotswolds.

At least I was now looking at *silent* cars. For what is the ruin of Broadway is the never-ending stream of through-traffic, the town being on the main route to Evesham and Stow, to Stratford and Cheltenham.

At nine that morning, we could have been in any major city, in the midst of rush hour – cars taking people to and from work, and on long journeys, tractors and wagons and farm machinery and, worst of all, huge container vehicles, of the length and weight that should be banned from taking *any* route running directly through *any* town, and allowed only on motorways.

By the time ten o'clock came, and the coaches and day-trippers had begun to arrive, there were traffic jams in all directions and the noise and fume level was as high as in any London street. I could not hear myself think. I had to lean towards the friend I was with to hear what she was saying. Crossing the road was a dangerous business, lorries thundering downhill merrily ignored the speed limit.

(Opposite) *Naunton in the Windrush Valley; traffic congestion in Broadway*

Broadway needs a by-pass. It is a scandal that it doesn't have one, and a nonsense, too, for the town generates prosperity for the region and the country. It deserves a return on its contribution to tourism, and its residents and visitors alike deserve to be able to enjoy this delightful place in as much peace as possible. For Broadway *is* delightful. I realised as I walked about, and as it grew busier and the shops opened, that it is not the tourists that spoil the town, but the through-traffic.

For years, it has been fashionable to sneer at Broadway because of its popularity, to dismiss it as a mere picture-postcard place, call it a tourist-trap and a rip-off town. To say that it is impossible to find a real shop there any longer, hard to buy a pound of butter or a dishcloth or a garden spade, only possible to buy expensive Scottish woollens, tacky gifts and souvenirs, cakes and chocolates; to say that all the antique dealers in the Midlands seem to have migrated to Broadway, attracted by so many visiting rich Americans; to say that, in short, Broadway is awful.

But Broadway is not. Alec Clifton Taylor wrote of it: 'What in fact one finds there, as all over the Cotswolds, are gentle variations of design and style, bound together into a harmonious unity by the use of the same lovely stone throughout.' Indeed, there are houses here built in that mellow, honey-coloured Guiting stone as early as the fourteenth century; houses from the Tudor age, and there are many that date from the eighteenth century. Broadway was one of the first Cotswold villages to attract many of the thoroughly prosperous families so it has more than its fair share of imposing houses, but there are numerous more modest domestic buildings too. Walk down one of the many little side alleyways that lead off the main street, and you find tiny, perfect cottages and neat little terraces tucked away behind cobbled and usually flowery courtyards.

Broadway, quiet in the evening light

Broadway is as fine a showplace for the talents and skills of local English builders through several centuries as anywhere in the country. You could compile a rich notebook of the details alone, of doorways and windows, of roofs, of gateposts, of porches. The trees that line the long street on both sides give shade and soften the line of the stone. The shop fronts have, on the whole, been well designed so that ugly modern signs and fascias do not obtrude. The gardens are all lovingly cared for. And it is only fair to say that Broadway is full of gift shops and tea shops because that is what the great majority of visitors ask for in such a place. Who has the right to sneer at people who want to stroll up the street, window-shopping and choosing presents, and then sit down among the chintz and horse-brasses to an excellent Cotswold cream tea? The company is good humoured and content, most of the goods on sale are of high quality and the antiques are usually genuine.

I don't like over-crowded towns, and I like the mighty roar of Broadway's traffic even less. I think if I really do want to have the place to myself, I must get up and drive there to arrive not later than five-thirty on a spring or autumn morning.

And when Broadway *does*, at last, get its by-pass – and really it seems to be one of the easiest places in the country around which to build a by-pass road – then those who want to get on their way fast will not have the frustration of a slow trail through the traffic jams of the little town, whilst those who want to come here and stay to appreciate its beauties will be able to do so.

But however crowded Broadway may be, and however long it may take you to get through it, peace and quiet and rural isolation are close by. Even on a warm day in full summer, when Broadway is at its worst, a few minutes away in either direction, you may walk among meadows and see no one and hear nothing but the bleating of sheep.

A little over a mile from Broadway lies the village of Buckland – you take the A.46 Cheltenham road, and turn off it, to the left. There are a number of country lanes like this, at first going along the flat, but soon beginning to climb quite steeply up, clefting the Cotswold ridge. At its highest points, above Snowshill and beside Broadway Tower, the ridge reaches over 1,000 feet, but below nestle small villages, beside streams, among woods and sheep-grazed meadows. Some are better known than others, but none is ever very crowded.

And the best and most tranquil of them is Buckland. It boasts one of the smartest country house hotels in the region now, and some of the old cottages and farm buildings have been converted for holiday letting. It has a magnificent early fifteenth-century rectory – the oldest in the county and still in use – and a lovely church. It has a stream trickling down from the hills above, under small stepping-stone bridges following the line of the lane beside the stone houses. It is, I think, a perfect place. Yet, on a summer's afternoon, when Broadway was as busy as it can ever be, Buckland lay still and empty and quiet under the sun.

I walked along the lane as it slopes up and winds round, and the wind stirred the tree tops and the sheep bleated, and in the lake at the front of the handsome house at the head of the village, a fish plopped. No other noise except the occasional ring of a hammer on stone where the masons were working on a house and the note sounded all the way up the quiet valley. If it is like this here in high summer, how utterly silent and undisturbed Buckland will lie through the snows of winter. When the cottages are empty of their holiday visitors and the hotel is closed, there are precious few residents left, for this is only a hamlet. There is no shop, no pub, no meeting place apart from the church. Walk uphill, and away from the main road, and you can be quite alone, in high, open country with the whole Vale of Evesham and the plain that stretches to Stratford at your feet, and only the bleating sheep and the winds that blow very cold up here, for company.

In summer, too, it seems to me that Buckland has

managed to welcome its visitors without giving itself over to them, or to spoil and change the essential nature of this place. If you stayed here, for a weekend or a week or a season, you would have to slip into the village and become part of it. And you would have to enjoy quietness.

It's hard to put a finger on the exact nature of the charm Buckland has for me, to say why I find that elusive spirit of the Cotswolds here, as I find it in only a handful of other places. It isn't architecturally perfect, but it has some good things. Its position is good but not uniquely so. The church has some treasures – what Cotswold church does not? – and best of all is the exquisite wood-panelled and painted roof, recently completely cleaned.

For all its slightness and smallness, it is as a whole that Buckland delights rather than for any individual splendour. I think that's true of most of the best Cotswold places – the atmosphere, the harmony of buildings and landscape, the quietness, the rightness of a group of buildings set together, the way the fields and woods come right up to the door to form a backdrop and lend a pleasing perspective.

From Buckland, drive back onto the main road leading to Cheltenham, and a few hundred yards on, take another left turn, to climb up again through quite deep woodland, and shady tree-lined lanes, first to the picture-book village of Stanton and, from there, following the line of the Cotswold Way, to Stanway.

Stanton has been much written about. It is much photographed, much praised – indeed, it is often called the most exquisite, the most perfect village in the Cotswolds, and I suppose, for that very reason, I resist it, just as I have always resisted that film-set which is Castle Combe near Bath.

Stanton is too perfect, too neat, there is nothing out of place. And so it is self-conscious, like a woman who has always been told how beautiful she is. There is something slightly artificial and lifeless about this im-

Buckland

maculately proportioned street of utterly Cotswold stone houses.

I suppose what I am looking for is some note of incongruity, some evidence that a place is breathing, able to change, as human life changes. The ultimate fate of a perfectly preserved village is to be taken over by the National Trust, and become like Lacock, unreal, trapped forever in a time-warp, dead.

No, Stanton is not dead. I saw children tumbling on a corner and people drinking outside the pub in the sun, and a van delivering sausages to the village shop, and the notice-board was crammed with details of

(Top) *The village street of Stanton;* (bottom) *The church of St Peter, Stanway, and the Jacobean gateway to Stanway House.* (Opposite) *Stanway village in November*

The cricket pavilion at Stanway

activities and social events. And even in July, there was a strange lack of obvious tourists.

Stanway had a few, taking photographs of the remarkable Jacobean gatehouse to Stanway House – it has strangely curved gables, with stone scallop-shells on top, and a triumphal sort of arch. This whole corner of the village that sits below thick wooded hills is architecturally imposing and rather surprising, too. Golden-stoned, all seems so grand for such a secluded and modest spot. As well as the great Elizabethan manor, there is a tithe barn and the vicarage and all complement one another, and there is nothing mean or plebeian about any of them.

But what I like best of all about Stanway is its cricket pitch, with the most delightful wooden pavilion I've seen – raised up above the ground on staddle stones. From the benches on the veranda, you have a fine view not only of a fine field but of the lovely trees that fringe it and, through the gap between them, of the open countryside stretching far away.

Last time I was there, I sat for a while on my own, hearing the echoes of pairs of studded boots going down the steps onto the pitch, and returning more heavily; smelling the strange smell, an amalgam of whitening and linseed oil and tea-urn which is common to all cricket pavilions; hearing the ghostly clapping, and the creak and clang of the tin numbers swinging over on the scoreboard, and the crack of a glorious six lifted high, high over the roof, into the blue Cotswold sky. The joy of cricket is as much in the memory and the imagination as in the match itself, most of all in a place like Stanway, on an afternoon when I had the whole place, field and pavilion, quite to myself.

I had Hailes Abbey to myself that day, too, and if Stanway was thronged with a host of phantom cricketers, at Hailes there were the ghosts of as many silent monks who had lived and worked and prayed in this beautiful and most tranquil place, down all the years from the thirteenth century to the Dissolution. There are never many people here, and those who do come seem to be affected by the quietness and holiness of the place, so that no one makes any noise, or shouts or rushes about.

On late afternoons, when the shadows of the ruined stone walls lengthen across the grass, and the birds fly high, Hailes Abbey is a place for sitting and thinking. There are good wooden benches so placed that you can look up the line of the gently rising hills around, dotted about with great trees. The turf is soft to walk on, and the ruins are spacious and open to the sky. I only wish there were one or two plain and unobtrusive but helpful signs, indicating that here, you are standing in the chapter house or the cloister or the abbey kitchen – it would give a greater sense of how the place must once have been.

Hailes Abbey is special. I think I like it best in winter when the trees are bare. It breathes the past, but it is not melancholy, it is a reminder of the violence done to such holy places, but the piety and peace of earlier, more reverent times have prevailed,

The ruins of Hailes Abbey

and now the atmosphere is wholly good. For those who do not care for churches, and who feel claustrophobic inside them, or who don't want to attend services but like to have a place and a space in which to pray, or to reflect prayerfully, the ruins of an abbey in such a beautiful part of the countryside as Hailes will serve them well.

But even those unattracted by churches should go into the little one just across the lane from Hailes Abbey. It was built in the twelfth century, one hundred years before the Abbey itself. It is very plain and very small, and very light because of the plain glass in its windows. It has some of the best wall-paintings in the Cotswolds on its white-washed walls – graceful figures of St Catherine and St Margaret, a St Christopher crossing the water carrying the Christ Child, and some figures from a bestiary, but most startling and moving of all is the hunting scene, on the south wall of the nave. Why it should be here, in a church, who can tell? It is a beautiful, primitive thing, with such life and quickness and movement about it that it must have been simply that the artist, presented with a bare wall and full of excitement at the idea of such a scene, drew away as joyfully and freely as a small child draws with a crayon on such a great white surface. The huntsman, blowing his horn, carries a shield; the greyhounds race, straining and panting, ahead of him, to the spot where a hare, crouched and frozen with terror, is at bay under the slender boughs of a bare tree. Perhaps it is a picture with a moral, perhaps the artist was appalled by the cruelty and bloodthirstiness of the sport and painted his picture in a church as a cry to God for vengeance on behalf of all such poor hunted creatures.

Perhaps that is an unlikely and sentimental thought, but I know that I love the interior of Hailes' small, pale church as well as I love any other in the Cotswolds,

12th-century wall-painting in Hailes church

along with that very similar, light, bare, beautiful church in the middle of the water meadows of the Windrush, St Oswald's at Widford.

In both, there is such a sense of the quiet and the prayer, of the deeply-held beliefs and true values of the past, an absence of show, and a closeness to sky and fields that lie beyond. At Hailes, that is all of a piece with the ruins of the monastery, too, so that you cannot help but be touched and restored by it.

There is another way leading to peace and quiet and wonderful countryside that runs out of busy Broadway. It takes you into the high places where, in winter, the snows drive across the fields and pile high, isolating the farms and hamlets that huddle inwards against the wind. Up here, some of the roads become single-track, and it is wonderful for walking. You feel as if you are on the roof of the world, with only the sheep and birds for company.

Take the road out of Broadway signposted to Snowshill; it runs first through that part of the village called Bury End in which there are some large and beautiful houses. There is also, on the left, the Victorian church of St Michael – but better to save church visiting for a rarer treat, a mile out as the road runs into fields. Here, on the right, is the original parish church, dedicated to St Eadburgha. It is set, as Cotswold country churches so often are, like a jewel in perfect surroundings, with the open, sheep-filled meadows beyond, climbing away up onto the escarpment, and with trees that soften the outlook but are not dark and close and claustrophobic.

St Eadburgha's is Norman, with later additions, and it reminds me very much of one of my most favourite churches in England – All Saints at Burton Dassett in Warwickshire. It is quite large and rather bare, with wonderful arches and, most charming of all, its bell-ropes hang gracefully down into a small central well, like a sort of courtyard, so that the ringers are not shut away as they perform their strange, patterned ritual,

which has always seemed to me one of the most delightful, creative and wholly *good* activities possible.

St Eadburgha's is only open during the summer months when there is Sunday Evensong, and I suppose, in view of its isolation from the village and the cost of heating old stone churches, that is entirely understandable. Yet it doesn't give off any air of deadness or neglect. It must simply hibernate peacefully through each winter, and then be made ready for sunlight and open doors and visitors again. It feels loved and cared for, and friendly. And its graveyard assumes a place in my private collection of those which are particularly pleasing places to wander about and sit quietly in.

If you are a walker, you can leave your car here, and cross the fields, climbing more and more steeply, up to Broadway Country Park which is what now surrounds Broadway Tower. The name is rather off-putting but it is only on fine summer days and at weekends that the Country Park is full of the world and his wife having their picnics. If you are hardy enough, go in winter and take a flask of hot soup; stand on one of the grassy mounds, with the bitter wind blowing in your face, and see half of middle-England lying at your feet, and even all the way to Wales. The Tower itself is a folly. It is made of darker stuff than the sunlit stone out of which Broadway itself is built, so that it looks medieval and slightly brooding and sinister against the sky. In fact, it was only put there in 1800 so that the Earl of Coventry could show off to his wife the extent of the lands he owned. Climb to the top and, with the help of a telescope, you can see up to twelve counties (depending upon how you arrange your counties, pre- or post-1974), round a full 190 degrees – it's fun ticking them off!

The Country Park itself has been pleasantly fitted out, with picnic tables on mounds and, in little dips of the field, some well-designed play equipment for children. Giant chessmen, which seem to be used in all manner of games except the game of chess, and an enclosure with farm animals. There are nature trails,

St Eadburgha's church

too, and an excellent barn-restaurant which serves the best egg sandwiches I've ever eaten!

If you have visited Broadway Country Park with young children, and perhaps had a picnic there, you could then extend the day's expedition by visiting the Cotswold Farm Park, a few miles to the south, near the village of Guiting Power.

Here, in an informal blend of fields and converted barns, is the home of many rare British breeds of farm animal, from the famous Cotswold sheep to Gloucester Old Spot pigs, taking in cattle, goats and poultry on the way. It's a happy place, with small animals to be fed, swings and slides to play on, and good teas too. Afterwards, you can walk across the rough open fields which surround the animal areas, and enjoy the fresh winds that always seem to blow up here.

Both here and Broadway Country Park are fine for a family outing; they won't appeal to everyone but, of

their kind, they are first-class, and for children who spend their days in the town or on the flat, they provide an exhilarating experience of high places and bracing fresh air.

From the Broadway Tower, by car or on foot, take the back way, all along the heights, to Snowshill, one of the highest villages in the Cotswolds. The stone of the houses is much greyer here, adding to the slightly austere, bleak air of the place – the cottages are quite close together, set around a green sloping away from the church. From odd corners, you can look across the fields and lanes that drop down to the narrow wooded valleys far below. Snowshill is most visited for its manor, which is in the hands of the National Trust.

I first visited it one late September day, twenty-five years ago. The lanes leading to Snowshill were quite empty, the village itself was silent. It was late afternoon, the day was grey and unseasonably cold and windy, with rain blowing in gusts into my face. Snowshill didn't have so many visitors in those days – no one I mentioned it to had even heard of it – and, in any case, it was the end of the season. I'm not sure what I expected but I wasn't prepared for what I found at Snowshill Manor. And if ever I visited a haunted house, it was this, though it was only after-

Snowshill nestles beneath the hill

wards that I heard the stories about it and looked up others in the local history books.

From the outside it is unremarkable – that is, it is a typical Cotswold manor house dating from about 1500, built of the local stone, and in a beautiful situation, surrounded by pretty gardens.

Inside it is very odd indeed, odd and distinctly sinister – or so I found it that dark day as all alone I wandered in and out of its rooms, to the echo of my own footsteps. It contains an eccentric collection of all manner of incongruous curios, formed by the last owner, now dead, called Charles Wade. There were early toys and weird waxwork dolls, stiffly-costumed

Snowshill village and Church of St Barnabas

figures, innumerable softly ticking clocks and, horrible and startling in the dim rooms, models of Japanese Samurai warriors and suits of armour.

I was so affected by it, my imagination half-fascinated, half-repelled, that I couldn't get it out of my mind and it began to haunt me in dark dreams until, some years later, I exorcised it by amalgamating it in two rather peculiar short stories. After that, I didn't think of Snowshill again until I was back in the village one recent day in December. The houses, the dry-stone walls, the sloping green, the views of the countryside, all seemed exactly the same. The Manor wasn't open, and I wouldn't have gone in, in any case. Such places, which have become part of my own inner landscape and have entwined themselves in my fictions, are best left, like certain memories, undisturbed. It was only a few weeks later that I sat in a small Cotswold front room and listened to some more stories of ghostly happenings and peculiar experiences at Snowshill, from someone who had worked there – and I wasn't at all surprised!

Nowadays Snowshill is much visited, and perhaps the passage of so many people going cheerfully about the gardens and exploring the house has let fresh air into the place, and swept away the ghosts. But the

St Mary, Temple Guiting; (opposite) *Guiting Power seen across the fields*

Japanese suits of armour and the eerie dolls and the rest of the curious collection are still there, and at twilight, or on grey mornings of lowering skies, I would prefer not to be alone there.

But go back outside again and you are close to the sky and with high open spaces all around and below.

From Snowshill, you can go in many Cotswold directions, and the landscape will change with every other mile. Drive a bit to the west, across the flat plain below the ridge, and you are out of the Cotswolds altogether and in the rich orchard and farmland of the Vale of Evesham. North-eastwards lies the Shakespeare country.

But I like to leave Snowshill and go due south, gently dropping down to the lovely, tree-filled, shady valley of the little Windrush that flows through the hamlets of Cutsdean and Ford to Temple Guiting. This is a rather winding and spread-eagled village whose church, named after the Knights Templars, is one of the handsomest in the Cotswolds when viewed from across the parkland that surrounds it. It has a

fine, dominating tower and the body of the nave stands broad and high. And there is a beautiful grassy grave-yard. Stand here, and look to the beech and ash, oak and lime trees in full-skirted splendour beyond. Inside, the church has the cold formality of the similar heavily eighteenth-century one at Blockley, ten miles or so away – you feel as if you are being kept at arm's length, and that muddy feet and country clothing would be inappropriate here.

A mile or so from here, on higher ground again, lie two of my most favourite Cotswold villages of all. The first I had visited at other seasons, but had rather forgotten how very good it was until I arrived in it again, one golden afternoon in high summer.

I complained earlier that I find the village of Stanton too perfect, too preserved, and in the *Shell Guide to Gloucestershire*, I see that the same criticism is made

of Guiting Power. 'It seems', the author writes, 'the deadly hand of a perfectionist has been at work.' How strange that I do not think this at all true! Guiting Power is absolutely right, not only in the beauty of its individual cottages and rows of small houses, grouped around the sloping green, but much more, as a simple whole. There isn't anything wrong, the roofs and stone walls, the doors and porches and windows and drip mouldings and gables and walls are all exactly right. But as I stood in the sun, looking round with the extreme satisfaction one can receive only from such absolute rightness of domestic architecture, I felt that here was a real, living, working village, not a piece of self-conscious conservation. Some small boys sat on top of a wall looking interestedly down on us; a tractor towing a hay-laden trailer lumbered through; the bell of the shop door pinged, a recalcitrant spaniel refused to obey orders. And down at the bottom of a leafy lane, grandparents dabbled the toes of a toddler in the cool clear water of a tiny dammed-up stream, and watched as he threw stones into the water and delighted at the splash.

It was a good place to be, with people going about their everyday business and enjoying the summer weather, and the stone walls looking as mellow as butter-and-honey. A pretty picture postcard – yes, but not only that, something solid and alive as well. I could live here, I thought, standing again on the green and looking around. I admire and enjoy many Cotswold places, but there aren't a lot I feel so sure about.

There is another, though, and that only a stone's throw-into-the-River-Windrush away. Curiously enough, I didn't know this village, had never particularly registered so much as the name on the map, until one day only a winter ago. It was the end of February, very cold, very bright. There had been heavy rain, filling up the rivers and streams and making them run fast, flooding fields, causing fords to overflow and become difficult to pass. But now the wind had got up, pushing away the rain-bearing clouds. It came cold

across the open fields, and we drove down from the hills in search of a pub with hot food and a good fire. For some time we had been unlucky – no food, or cold food, or tart notices banning walkers with muddy boots. I had the map, and time was ticking on to two, and still no lunch. We felt short tempered. 'Naunton,' I read out, 'a mile to the left. Let's try there.'

We tried, and with success. Naunton, about which I knew nothing, yielded a good pub, with hot home-cooked food and a fire and a horse tied up to a post outside while its rider chatted with friends at the bar.

By the time we had eaten and rested and were warm again, we were inevitably feeling well disposed towards hospitable Naunton, but walking from the pub along the village street, I began to realise that this was not just another good Cotswold place; it had that mysterious, magical combination of ingredients which made it special. On the right, going in the direction of the church, is a terrace of small cottages set back behind long front gardens with straight paths running up to the doors; that is especially good. A little further on and in a grassy clearing behind some old farm buildings, is the famous Naunton dovecote, erected in about 1660. It is deserted, crumbling to ruin but still beautiful with its four gabled stone walls, like a real cottage.

It seems extremely sad when any old and beautiful country building is left to decay and perhaps ultimately to collapse. Land can always be reclaimed, trees and hedgerows replanted and wildlife encouraged to return, though it may well take years of patient effort; nature will always get the upper hand again if allowed to do so. But buildings are irreplaceable in their original form once they have fallen or been pulled down, and every one is in some way unique. Castles and great houses are preserved at great cost, old houses are

(Opposite top) *Naunton's dovecote;* (bottom) *Early morning light on stubble fields*

protected, at least to some extent, by being listed. But the architectural beauty and character of the Cotswolds lies as much as anything in its numerous ancient workaday buildings, barns, stables, privies – and dovecotes. Individually, they may not be rare or very remarkable; collectively, they matter a great deal. Too many barns have been altered out of all recognition, and ruined by being badly converted into houses by architects with no visual sensitivity. Dovecotes are historic and lovely things, and no one will ever build them again. Perhaps conservation bodies are powerless to prevent neglect by private owners. Perhaps they should not be.

Then the road begins to climb. There are some new

houses, and a shop. And at the crest of the hill, on the left, the old Baptist chapel, with a path running around the side. We followed it into the old graveyard, very derelict, dipping steeply down, with long grass and some broken table-top tombs, and many sunken stones, and a few dark trees, yew and elder, and bushes. All the same, it is a romantic spot.

We looked down into the water meadows of the Windrush, and then up again, following the rise of the opposite slopes dotted with trees and the odd cottage. That would have been enough to make Naunton memorable, but there was more delight to come as we followed the road that drops again, bending round, as the Windrush bends, to a bridge with cottages on either side, and willows and water-plants, and the stream running clear over the stones on its narrow bed. Ahead, the church, set up on a slight slope. Following a path back along the line of the hill, we

---

(Below) *View from the Baptist chapel in Naunton across the Windrush Valley*

Above the Windrush Valley, near Naunton

stopped and looked across to where the houses of Naunton lie together, and there was the old grave-yard of the plain grey Baptist chapel. It was very cold, the air as clear as clear, the sky a brilliant wintry blue.

We returned to the car, drove back out of the village to the cross-roads with the road from Stow. We parked and then, on foot, climbed a steep hill between thick hedges. In the field close beside us, sheep with their lambs, bleating and fretting, moving away from us anxiously. Each ewe was numbered, her lambs were numbered on their backs to match. We looked through a gap, across wide, open sheep-scattered fields, to a narrow road which ran up from a farm beside a ford, like a silver-grey ribbon unwinding.

The wind cut keenly through the bare trees, and when we took the ribbon road and climbed high, high again above Naunton, it became stronger, pushing white clouds, like curds, fast across the sky. And from all around, borne on the wind, the crying of the sheep, the pervading sound of the Cotswolds, followed us through the gathering darkness of the afternoon as we made for home.

Village Life

(Top left) *Façades in Chipping Campden's high street;* (above) *cottage in Southrop with a flourishing vegetable garden and* (right) *the bus shelter in Hatherop.* (Opposite) *Cotswold cottages: the cottage in Duntisbourne Abbots has a more typical roof* (top) *than the thatched cottage in Broad Campden* (bottom)

6. Cheltenham

One of my happiest memories of Cheltenham was one October Sunday and, as so often, the back end was the best of the year. The morning had been unpromising, with low cloud and damp drizzle, and although the sun came out as I drove along the A.40 from Oxford, the day remained blurred at the edges, blue-violet-grey and hazy.

By lunch-time, it was warm, as warm as many an afternoon in high summer, but with that special precious, sweet warmth of autumn, golden and smoke-smelling. It was an afternoon to tempt people out of doors, for on days like this, so late in the year, every hour of sunshine and warmth is to be savoured, each fine Sunday might be the last before October slips downhill into the dank, drear and early dark of November and unmistakable winter.

Strolling about the avenues of Cheltenham on such a day was rather like being in Paris. The plane trees in the squares and the chestnut trees lining the wide, wide Promenade and gracing the park were fully on the turn, showing off the best of their red and copper and bronze and yellow-gold. The ground was littered with the green cases of conkers where they had burst open softly and given up their polished fruit to in-numerable small boys who dived after one and then another, while younger more timid children danced on the sidelines with excitement. And on pavements and about the pretty little courtyards, the young sat at tables, drinking sophisticated-looking drinks out of tall glasses, the smart, privileged, gilded young, with that air of nonchalance and fashion that the young have in Rome and Venice – and Paris.

Others, couples, the well-dressed middle-aged, window-shopped in the chic boutiques and glossy stores, or sat at other tables in the gardens of hotels, taking afternoon tea among the tubs of geraniums.

In the open spaces, the municipal parks and gardens with which the town is better endowed than any except Harrogate, mothers sat on benches and pushed prams to and fro, and watched the toddlers play; here little girls wheeled little prams, and old men slept in the sun.

I can think of few other places with such an atmosphere and spaciousness, so many trees fringing such elegant avenues, such stylish shops. Cheltenham is utterly different from any other place in the Cotswolds. Cirencester is county, old-fashioned, good-quality, understated, yet Cheltenham has become extremely fashionable and expensive, a designer-town, and all

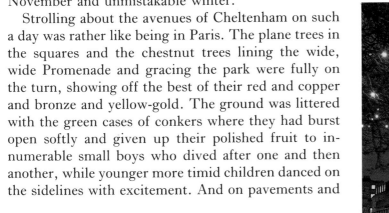

A November dawn on the Humblebee Wood road; (right) Christmas lights in Montpellier, Cheltenham

Regency buildings in Cheltenham

this based on solid foundations of handsome architecture and good buildings of graceful proportions.

It was not always so. In Victorian and Edwardian times, of course, Cheltenham was solidly middle-class and prosperous – hence all the villas in the leafy residential avenues west of Montpellier, so many now turned into offices, hotels and boarding houses for College girls and boys.

The town had a reputation for prosperity, Indian civil servants retired there, it was all a little like Leamington Spa – or, indeed, many another spa town, for that is what Cheltenham is. But during the years after the second war, it began to look very shoddy and shabby and down-at-heel as the money ran out and the pensions were devalued; then the façades of the houses flaked and stucco crumbled. 'Cheltenham,' a friend said, clearing up the house after an elderly aunt and uncle died, 'is not what it was.'

But these days, things are very different – the retired colonial civil servants and Army majors have gone, and money has come in, new money, and with it, taste; demand for the best in style and design, in clothes, furnishings, antiques, art. It is a pleasure to walk past all the new small shops in Montpellier at the north end of the Promenade, and find such individuality and originality – at a price, of course. The cheaper chain stores are all there in Cheltenham somewhere, but they have not forced out the small shop owners and restaurateurs.

There is a great deal happening in these lively and elegant streets, too. Cheltenham is proud of its music and literature festivals, while its National Hunt Festival in March brings another sort of style, and a stimulating variety of visitors. There is a good and enterprising theatre, the town has a history of housing some of the best schools in the country – and the green hills of the steep Cotswold ridge run down to the back door; you are away from the rather messy suburbs and into some of the most peaceful and beautiful villages, open fields, high hills, in minutes.

I spent an entirely happy afternoon here. One of the pleasures of life, which the English climate does not permit as often as the continental but which is therefore all the more to be relished, is the pleasure of strolling about the avenues and promenades, the squares and arcades of a handsome town, of sitting at a café table watching the world go by, of taking the sun and admiring the idiosyncratic floral effects achieved in parks by municipal gardeners.

Cheltenham, in the centre, is not large and, like all Regency towns, it is well and clearly laid out on a geometric principle. Walking around the centre takes no more than an hour or so at a moderate pace. England is rich in towns of a manageable size and good proportions, particularly those established in the Regency period. Cheltenham is not typical of the Cotswolds, it is a curiously anomalous, interesting, and visually and socially rewarding addition to them.

The Cotswolds are partly in Oxfordshire, and touch on the borders of Worcestershire and Wiltshire, and Avon, too, but for the most part, they are in Gloucestershire. Stand on Cleeve Hill, the highest natural point in the whole region, and you look across Cheltenham to the Vale of Gloucester, and to that city itself, standing on the River Severn.

And dominating Gloucester, rising out of it in glory, and visible for miles around, is the tower of Gloucester Cathedral. I think it is probably the finest in the country, though others will at once claim superiority for Wells, or Winchester. At any rate, Gloucester is my favourite, it is the one that speaks to me, and moves me most; its atmosphere is warm, and it isn't merely a tourist centre, stuffed full of treasures and yet lacking in spiritual identity.

Gloucester has had its heart turned to stone – or rather to multi-storey concrete and pedestrianised-neon, it is cheap and rather tawdry now, but the approaches

The fantasy clock designed by Kit Williams in the Regent Arcade, Cheltenham. On the hour, everything revolves, music plays and the fish blows real bubbles. (Opposite) *Old Gloucester*

to the cathedral and one or two last medieval streets are characterful enough.

And suddenly, in the midst of it all, there is that mighty building, and seen across the grass and quiet open spaces of the precinct all around, it should be unspoiled, dominant, awe-inspiring – and so it would be, except that the authorities have bowed down before that all-powerful god, the motor car, and allowed parking all over the cathedral square and in lines up

against the entrance so that the majesty, the whole line and rise of the great building is spoiled by the metal jungle. Some motor cars may be visually pleasing, individually; many motor cars en masse never ever are. They should be swept away from the cathedral precincts, and the way left free for those on foot only. The planners have ruined so much of Gloucester that the erection of yet another concrete car park will spoil nothing – and, indeed, if they had any sense and were willing to spend money, the cars could even, as in London, be banished underground.

But once you are inside Gloucester Cathedral, nothing can detract from its splendour. The great east window, the beautiful fan vaulting, the quiet perfection of the cloisters, the ambulatory, the monuments, the carving on the choir stalls – oh, everything, anything, take your pick of what you think is the greatest glory, it is all superb. And among the minor triumphs, don't pass by two monuments set into the north wall: one, dating from the eighteenth century, extravagant, poetic, romantic, moving, to the mother of a young family, who died in childbirth while at sea. The other, very recent, restrained and austere, but most harmoniously designed for its setting, to the late Duke of Beaufort who lived at Badminton House.

Many English cathedrals prompt feelings of respect, awe, piety, but Gloucester prompts love. It is a living place, it is quiet, it is profoundly beautiful, unrivalled

Gloucester Cathedral can be seen from miles around; (opposite) *inside the cloister gardens*

in the Cotswolds, unrivalled in the country. After all the small stone village churches, all the imposing and sometimes pompous wool churches of the market towns, in an area rich indeed in the best of ecclesiastical architecture from the eleventh century onwards, Gloucester comes as the summit, the climax to it all, a great Hallelujah Chorus of a church, exciting, proud – not to be missed.

From the centre of Cheltenham, it is only eight or so miles to Winchcombe across the spectacular top of the ridge, but you can take a rather more circuitous route and, on the way, discover a secret and most beautiful stretch of road, with some of the Cotswolds' best views over meadows and woodland to the opposite hills which then lead the eye gently, satisfyingly away to the horizon.

Leave Cheltenham by the A.40 Oxford road, but take the turning off it to the left, in the direction of Whittington. This is a strange small village with a number of very small terraced cottages fronting onto the street, many of which are empty and run-down, or even partly derelict, some of which are spruce and lived-in. The whole place has the air of partial neglect

The village of Whittington

(Above) *A November dawn on the Humblebee Wood road;* (below) *near Charlton Abbots*

Doorsteps in Winchcombe

above Brockhampton there is a fine view over the valley. Good villages, not much known or on the tourist beat, a mixture of old and modern – worth a detour.

From Brockhampton, the road climbs and dips like a switchback. It is best in winter, then no one much seems to come this way. When you come to woods on your left, stop and get out, stand beside any of the gates or gaps in the hedge, and below you are fields of sheep, or ploughed earth sloping gently away to the valley bottom, and then rising up again, steeply on the opposite side. There are good thick hedges, trees here and there, the roof of a barn, the line of a track. To the left, the dark, thick swathe of Humblebee Wood rises, behind which lies the superbly preserved prehistoric burial mound of Belas Knap. Further away, you can make out the grey walls and tower of Sudeley Castle.

Here the wind blows, the sheep cry, it is a bleak and lonely road. Yet I have sat in the shelter of the hedge and eaten a picnic in February, and the sun has warmed my face as well as it might in June. I love this road. I love the shape of the valley, the curve of the wood, the up-and-down dip and slope of field after field, the line of sky above the opposite ridge.

And at the end of it, turn right and you are at once into the noble hill-top town of Winchcombe which runs in a long line along the main road, and whose mansard roofs make such delightful patterns, as the streets slope steeply away. At Winchcombe, the houses on the hill have steps up to their doors, and the whole town seems shaped and organised by the rise and drop of the ground. Winchcombe is not so pretty or so touristy as Campden or Broadway, nor so bare and plain as Northleach. It is quite large and rather spread-eagled, but there is a compactness about the very centre which makes it manageable. Running down from the main street is an attractive lane leading to Sudeley Castle, a handsome fortress in lovely grounds with surviving buildings dating back to the fifteenth

and melancholy dilapidation that once marred the village of Great Barrington.

Beyond Whittington, turn left, and you pass close by the villages of Sevenhampton and Brockhampton, through which the upper stream of the River Coln runs. The houses and cottages are set along both slopes of the young river, and from the high point

Winchcombe, showing some black-and-white timbering

century and now carefully restored (and open to the public).

Until 1984, the church suffered from having an oak rood screen (albeit a fifteenth-century one) dividing chancel from nave, but it took its courage in both hands and had the screen moved to the back, so that now the whole building is both open and airy and lighter, yet also has come together as a whole.

Winchcombe is on the edge of the Cotswolds, you can tell as much by looking at the houses – for here,

black-and-white timbering creeps in, the building of the Shakespeare Country a few miles north. To the north-west lies the Vale of Evesham.

But turn your back on both, and look up the steep hill of the High Street, and what you see is Cotswold, the stone the colour of beeswax, the way the windows and doors are cut – you couldn't be anywhere else.

7. Tetbury

Before I ever saw Tetbury, I had two friends who went there and told me about it. The first was taking part in that curious and popular British sport – Royal-hunting. For Tetbury has become known, over the course of the past few years, not as a small, pleasant market town on the southern fringe of the Cotswolds so much as a Royal town, the nearest place to Highgrove House, home of the Prince and Princess of Wales. It was upon Tetbury that the international paparazzi descended after the newly-married couple had moved into their house, a mile outside the town, hoping to do some 'Di' spotting. It was to Tetbury hospital that the Lady Diana Spencer went on one of her first official visits after her engagement; she was photographed at Tetbury school and Tetbury church the following winter; it was to a Tetbury shop that she went to buy sweets, was pursued by photographers and fled. They used to camp on the grass verges outside Highgrove. I don't suppose they still do, but the whole thing brought unwelcome attention and a bit of money to Tetbury, and filled up the hotels and bars with newsmen. And with people like my friend, who spent a whole weekend there, anxious to look the place over, spot a princess or two, absorb the glamour.

Except, of course, that there isn't any. She came back disillusioned, saying that Tetbury was a 'one-eyed place', that there was nothing there, that she hadn't seen so much as a footman, and she simply couldn't understand why they'd gone to live there in the first place (probably just *because* of its quietness and plain-ness and small size, I would have thought. And because, if they do go shopping there, the press-men may take a lot of notice, but the people of Tetbury will very politely take none).

The second friend went to Tetbury to stay with a long-lost cousin, and liked it so much, found it so friendly, so pleasant, so full of her kind of people and opportunities for her sort of activity, that she bought a house there and lives in extremely happy retirement. Tetbury is, she says, 'just right', and above all, of manageable size – the typical market town, larger, with more amenities than a village, but less busy and noisy than the big Midlands town from which she came.

Two entirely different Tetburys, through the eyes of two very different people, looking for quite different things from it.

Certainly, if you arrive in Tetbury at five o'clock on an ordinary winter Friday afternoon, as I did, you

The Chipping Steps in Tetbury; (right) *Tetbury's Market Hall*

won't see any sign at all that it is a 'Royal town' – no notices of anything By Appointment, and certainly no pressmen. That is a great relief. Tetbury wisely doesn't boast of its royal connections, and doesn't trade on them.

It is a delightfully laid out town, with all its streets leading off the central market place, a pillared Market House of the same kind you see in other Cotswold towns – Chipping Campden, Minchinhampton – but nicer, I think, than all the rest. It was, of course, built for the wool markets during those great and prosperous medieval days since Tetbury is a wool town, like many another. Now, it's used for the Saturday stall-market, and for various other markets, as well – both in the arches below and the Town Hall above.

Whichever direction you walk in, you see, in Tetbury, some of the handsomest rows of houses in the Cotswolds. Many of them, in the steep streets that lead down hill out of the town to the south, and around the lovely square called The Chipping, are Georgian, with elegant, harmonious façades, tall windows, and all the details right – the doors, the doorknobs, the railings, the roofs. If you like simply looking at and admiring good domestic architecture, you will get a very great deal of pleasure from Tetbury; there's variety, everything goes well with everything else, but it isn't uniform or over-preserved or at all dull. There are odd quirky details, sudden incongruities, changes of line, of building material, of size – though there is scarcely anything out of scale.

The Chipping is spoiled because it is the car park. I wish they'd clear it and put cars into a park in the modern, functional bit, around by the fire station, so that the beautiful houses and the perfect proportions of the square could be enjoyed by themselves.

The shops are the right scale in Tetbury, too, all of them small, all individual. There are a few antique

A view over a typical lichen-encrusted Cotswold wall to St Mary's church, Tetbury

shops on Long Street, but not so many that the town has lost its identity as a real place – you can buy clothes and food and books and newspapers, and pots and pans and garden forks in Tetbury, as well as gifts, an oak dresser, or a Victorian watercolour.

The church is very surprising. Its spire can be seen, slender, light, rising up from the many- and high-windowed body, for miles around. Inside, it seems huge, airy, lofty, almost cathedral-like – and it is pure Gothic, not a barn-like medieval stone church, nor a great wool church like those at Campden and Northleach.

St Mary's is one of the first Gothic Revival churches, completed in 1781, and replacing a medieval one on the same site. It has box pews, and the windows, because they are so very large, make it feel extremely spacious. And, most curious and enjoyable of all, it has a sort of outer ambulatory – a cloister-like corridor running round the outside of the nave, and doors through which you can step directly into the pews. It's all rather theatrical and very unexpected in the middle of the Cotswolds; when I'd got used to it, I liked it a great deal.

As, indeed, I greatly like Tetbury. I like its atmosphere, the feel of the place, its layout, its design, its aspect and the way it gets on with its business. It is friendly and doesn't give itself airs – even though the hotel in the market place is called the Snooty Fox.

A few miles south-east of Tetbury lies Malmesbury which is firmly in Wiltshire and out of the Cotswolds, and the countryside immediately surrounding the town is not very interesting, with flat fields and straight roads.

Higher ground lies to the west, where the edge of the Cotswold Hills drops away finally towards the Severn. This little area is sometimes included in guide-books to the Cotswolds, and sometimes is not. And I can see exactly why there is confusion. Wotton-under-Edge, and the valley which leads up from it

towards Dursley and Nailsworth is, literally, under-the-edge of the ridge of the Cotswold Hills. It lies on the other side looking towards the Vale of Berkeley and the River Severn and, in many ways, neither the town itself nor the surrounding countryside *feels* Cotswold to me. And yet . . . and yet . . . there is something that makes me want to include Wotton-under-Edge – and the best reason of all is that it is such a pleasing place, unexpectedly large, set out on a steep hill, and running down to the flat plain below; a very un-touristy, *real* sort of town.

The outer bands, as it were, contain much serviceable, uninteresting modern housing but the central complex of streets is a wholly delightful mixture of plain, painted seventeenth- and eighteenth-century houses, very much like those in Cirencester, some traditional and earlier stone cottages, and one or two unusual and rather different buildings. As you climb the steep hill of the main street, you see rising ahead of you the curious cupola of Tolsey House, an eighteenth-century oddity which has a dragon for a weathervane, and adds a happy note of visual incongruity.

But the best bit of Wotton-under-Edge is a set of

Weathervane on Tolsey House in Wotton-under-Edge

Owlpen Manor and church

buildings in Church Street. Hugh Perry's Almshouses are entered through an archway. Once you pass down the little passage, you come out into what feels exactly like a tiny Oxford college quadrangle. It is square and cobbled. The houses, with doorways and staircases just like those in a college, all open out into this central courtyard. And set in the middle of it, up against a stone wall, are two wooden benches. I sat on one, in the sun. It was very quiet – but from one of the houses, a radio played faintly, in another hung a bird in a cage. And I thought this would be a perfect place in which to end your days – independent, and yet sheltered. Part of a community, yet with your own front door. Peaceful, yet in the centre of the town so that you could still go out to the shops, and be easily visited. And with a bench on which to sit and string your beans and chat to your friends.

And the wall against which the bench rested was the outside wall of a very, very small chapel, plain and simple within, very much part of the group of buildings.

To the north of Wotton-under-Edge, several valleys plunge deep into the Cotswold ridge, with steep slopes, narrow lanes, fields aslant, and dense woods. Penetrate to the heart of any of them and you are in a secluded, secret world which feels far from anywhere, and out of which you have to climb and clamber, perilously. In the heart of one of them lies the tiny hamlet of Owlpen – with a manor house, a church, a farm or two, a few cottages.

Looked at from the other side of the valley, Owlpen is snug, pretty, isolated. On a sunny, breezy spring day, when the leaves on the trees are dancing, it's a lovely place, but on a wet autumn day of lowering cloud and dismal damp, Owlpen changes its character and becomes sinister, closed-in, dark. The church has a gloomy, sloping graveyard, the trees press in around the manor house.

The spirit of the Cotswolds is a strange thing, as changeable as the weather, its mood is often sombre. In these little valleys, it is undoubtedly present, but shadowy, strange, and occasionally disturbing.

Returning to Tetbury, if you want to go back into the Cotswolds proper, you can take either the main A.433 north-east to Cirencester, or go up the road running almost due north, the one which takes you past another Royal house, Gatcombe Park, up to one of my favourite small towns in the whole of the Cotswolds – Minchinhampton.

But before you reach it, if you turn right off the road and follow signs to Cherington, you will come to a couple of exactly the kind of little-known, out-of-the-way places that make all of the Cotswolds special.

There's nothing very remarkable about Cherington; I haven't seen it highlighted in any of the guide-books I've come across. You approach the little village itself via an extremely steep road that drops down through woods. At the bottom, there lies a pond.

On the day I went, there was frost and ice in all the ditches, the grass in the cold dark bottom was white. The air was absolutely still, and the sky, high above my head, seen through the tree tops, was brittle blue. I'd been told that there was always a heron on the Cherington pond. I waited a long time, staring at tree stumps near the water. Herons often disguise themselves as tree stumps, but there was no bird, nothing moved or stirred. Then, from the other side of the water, on a track through the woods, the sound of a dog barking and being called several times to heel, and the noise of the bark rang round like a gun shot. The

Cherington pond

voice was several hundred yards away but came across the clear, cold, silent air as if the man and his dog were within reach of my hand. It felt mysterious, not eerie, just a bit ghostly.

I went on to Cherington. A high stone wall curves round on the right of the road. Opposite is as delightful a row of cottages as you might find in any of the much-visited tourist spots; low, stone-built, with a perfect line of roofs and, in the middle of them, the post office with the post van drawn up outside. I went in, expecting to find an all-purpose village shop – but there, in what was really the front parlour of the house, was simply the post-office counter with scales and stamps and posters about Datapost and Giro.

The next time I went to Cherington, it was June, a warm Sunday afternoon, and there was a cricket match in play. I parked at the edge of the field, under a tree, and watched a few overs – a smashing four – and another – a good fast bowler – a nifty bit of fielding and a swift throw in – out! Ah well.

Down some more narrow, empty lanes. A stretch of beautiful parkland, the front of a handsome house glimpsed at the end of a long drive. I stopped again. There was birdsong. No cars, no people. I leaned on a gate for a bit, thinking that good parkland with mature trees dotted about in it is one of the excellencies of England, and that, even in the middle of summer, only a few miles from main roads and market towns, you can feel like the only person in a country of your own imagining.

A few hundred yards further on, driving between low hedges fringing the cornfields, a family of baby stoats played together, jumping, tumbling, rolling over and over like all litters of young creatures – right in the very middle of the road. I got out of the car, crept towards them, managed to take a photograph of them – and a second – before they suddenly sensed me, and leaped away into the long grass of the ditch.

After that, I came to the small village of Rodmarton. There isn't anything very remarkable here. A village

(Above) *Cherington village has one of the many attractive post offices in the Cotswolds;* (opposite) *view across to Minchinhampton and Holy Trinity Church*

Minchinhampton. (Above) *The Ram Inn and market square;* (right) *the high street*

green with a few Cotswold stone houses round about. A rather ugly little church. A row of modest cottages on the left, with neat front gardens, gables, porches all in a line. And a stone bus shelter that looks like a miniature Cotswold barn, with a mossy, tiled roof. A few builders were working on a house but it was so quiet, the chink of the trowel on stone echoed all around. Otherwise, Rodmarton was empty. An unassuming place, entirely representative of many a good Cotswold village off the beaten track.

And so, back to Minchinhampton. In its way, that, too, is unassuming – and utterly right. It presents a uniform, harmonious appearance because it is almost entirely built of a soft grey limestone. There is a very long street, leading from south to north and, crossing it, another which runs up to the Market House. The houses that line both roads belong to the sixteenth, seventeenth and eighteenth centuries but because of the uniformity of the building stone they seem to belong much more closely to one another in period. They are good houses, strong-looking, solid, plain, and there are a lot of them, packing the lanes that lead downhill away from the centre. There is plenty of new building, too – Minchinhampton is a large place now.

Early morning on Minchinhampton Common

I had hot chocolate in the tea shop in the main street, one bitterly cold Saturday morning. It was packed, everyone was coming into town to shop. But when I looked out of the window, all I could see was a long string of horses going by the window, on their way to or from exercise on Minchinhampton Common – horses are part of the everyday scenery in the Cotswolds.

The Common – now owned by the National Trust – is a strange place, a mile out of the town itself; wide, open, humpy-bumpy downland, crossed by narrow, straight roads where horses mingle with grazing cows and sheep, and at the weekends with kite flyers, picnickers, golfers and strollers to the two pubs. It ought to be a bleak, wild, lonely place, but it's crowded, a sort of unofficial recreation ground and country park which stands high above the plain, with views all around.

The best time to come here would be at dawn on a winter's morning, with the red sun rising out of a misty sky and a line of horses galloping with smoking breath along the horizon, and not another soul in sight.

From Minchinhampton Common, you can go in one direction and all but fall off the edge of the Cotswolds completely. The road that drops down through the village of Box, towards Nailsworth, is extremely steep and very winding and I should not care to descend it in ice and snow. But Box is pretty, hanging on by its fingertips, a genteel little village whose houses have some dramatic views over the mill valley below.

Nailsworth is not attractive nowadays – it's a small,

messy town full of old mills, with an honourable industrial history. The place once hummed with the busy workings of the cloth trade, but the dark Satanic mills stand silent, either derelict or put to other uses. The steep hillsides are lined with the terraced cottages built for the cloth workers, smartened up now and hemmed in by modern developments. Nailsworth is still busy, but it has lost most of its non-Conformist Victorian character.

Go north from Minchinhampton, and you drop down from the airy heights again, into the Golden Valley which follows the River Frome and old Thames and Severn Canal to Stroud. Like Nailsworth, Stroud is part of the industrial scene in the Cotswolds. It was the very heart of the cloth-making industry and the villages that lie along the Golden Valley were also the homes of the many hundreds of workers – weavers and dyers – who created its prosperity.

It is not, I have to say, an area I like – because I don't like valleys with houses built up on steep sides, rising above me. I feel hemmed in by them. I long to get out, up onto the high roads and open spaces, closer to the sky.

A place like Chalford, whose little lanes are as steep as those of some Cornish fishing villages, fills me with a sort of claustrophobic dread. Others, I am sure, will not feel it and, certainly, the Golden Valley from Stroud is worth visiting just because it is so very different from anywhere else in the Cotswolds, with a history, an architecture, a landscape, an identity and an atmosphere that are quite unique.

And at the far end of the Golden Valley lies a very special place, a strange, quiet village called Sapperton which has one of the most beautiful situations in the Cotswolds. But, for one particular reason to do with that situation, I think of Sapperton in the same breath, as it were, as the village of Coates – and both of them as belonging most naturally to the nearby market town of Cirencester.

The Golden Valley; view towards Stroud

The Harvest

(Above) *Cornfield near Middle Duntisbourne and* (opposite) *Harvesting near Broad Campden*

8. Cirencester

A favourite game of mine is, 'If I did not live in an Oxfordshire village, where else would I like to be?' I come up with as many different answers as there are months in the year, and England is scattered with 'favourite houses' in which I feel I could happily settle.

But although I want to be in the country, I would also always like to live within reach of a good English market town – not too small a one, with too few shops and other facilities, nor too given-over to tourism, nor so large as to lose its essential market-town character.

And time and again, I come back to Cirencester as being the perfect town, of exactly the right size. It seems to me as handsome, as well laid-out, and yet as compact a town as can be found. Its situation is ideal, it looks right, it has a delightful atmosphere, a good feel to it, and it contains everything one could possibly need and all within walking distance.

It is also, nowadays, extremely fashionable. Cirencester is the market town for a very prosperous area of the Cotswolds. Its surrounding villages are select and beautiful, its farmland rich and productive, its houses command prices as high as anywhere else in the country outside the capital. The M.4 motorway has made weekend commuting easier and brought further prosperity. It is smart to live near Cirencester. The Royal Agricultural College trains the sons of gentlemen farmers to take over the family land – as well as those of more modest expectations – and has given a mildly Hooray-Henry image to the town. Royal Gloucestershire is nearby. Polo is played in Cirencester Park.

Yet, walk about Cirencester, browse in the market, shop in the many fine, individual shops, stroll in the Abbey grounds and in Cirencester Park itself, go into the church which has the feel of a cathedral – and you will not particularly notice or be put off by any snobbish air.

The market square is one of the most pleasing I know; its seventeenth-, eighteenth- and nineteenth-century houses, with their façades painted sugar-almond colours, are a perfect amalgam of modesty and elegance. The windows are so good, and the doors, and look up – there is such a nice roof-line all around; there are a few jarring notes on the shop façades, but for the most part, all the fascias have been done with restrained good taste.

(Opposite) *Market day in Cirencester;* (right) *Cirencester's church tower, and façades in the market square*

The chalkboards in the image read:

LOCH FYNE KIPPERS

THE ORIGINAL GLOUCESTER SAUSAGE £1·55 LB

SMOKED SALMON THE VERY BEST

PHEASANTS PARTRIDGE WILD DUCK AND LITTLE CHILDREN IF THEY RUB OUT THIS BOARD

On market day, the striped canvas awnings, like a conglomeration of umbrellas packed together in the centre of the square, are incongruous – but they bring the place alive, they have all the gaiety and temporary, slightly tawdry charm of a street fair.

I suppose the heart of any town is its shopping centre and the shops in Cirencester are very good; old-established quality butchers, wine merchants and gentlemen's outfitters are cheek by jowl with modern chain stores, but the latter are on the right scale for the town. Away from the main square, newer pedestrian precincts and arcades seem to be always busy.

You can learn a lot about the place from an hour or two spent here on market day, in and around the stalls and shops, where farmers' wives rub shoulders with county ladies, Range Rovers are parked next to very old Morris Minors, people buying hunting gear and Barbour jackets meet up with others looking for bargain underwear on the market stalls.

In much earlier times, the heart of the town was the church and that, too, is a step across the street, dominating the market square, just as its tower dominates the view for miles around. The best of it is the south porch with its breathtaking fan vaulting. Inside, St John the Baptist is imposing, impressive – and rather cold, not a church you can easily feel at home in or on familiar terms with, but magnificent nonetheless.

A good town must always have the countryside on its doorstep, and that is certainly true of Cirencester, but it should also contain green open spaces within its own precincts. Many towns have a park, but few can boast such marvellous ones as Cirencester Park, five square miles of open but formal parkland stretching as far as Sapperton, and always open to the public. The

trees are as good as any in England. And beside the church, the green lawns of the abbey grounds lead down to the river on which the swans gracefully glide – and not far away, the rolling Cotswold countryside.

A great deal has been made in recent years of the Roman past of the Cotswolds; archaeologically, the area around Cirencester, as well as the town itself, is of considerable importance – and tourists and school-children alike are being made very conscious of Roman villas, mosaics, pottery fragments – the glories of the Roman occupation of England uncovered in this corner of the Cotswolds.

If you are interested, the best place to go is certainly the Corinium Museum in Cirencester. Museums are amazing places, now all the dust and dullness have long been swept away. Corinium is splendid; it illumi-nates, unveils, explains the past of the town and the surrounding area; its cool, carefully-lit rooms and corridors are a pleasure to walk in, its displays are clear and good to look at, as well as interesting. To anyone like me, whose sense of history is defective, a museum like this is a revelation, and a godsend.

Yes, I should be glad to live near Cirencester, there is nothing about it – except the new road on the outskirts – that I dislike or that strikes the wrong note. There is no air of small-town fustiness, nothing mean about it – every prospect pleases indeed.

Roads emanate from Cirencester like the spokes of a wheel and being in several cases Roman roads, they are fine, straight ones and I like their Roman names a good deal better than their modern numbers.

Outside the town, there is a perfect fork. The left-hand prong, going north-north-east, is the Fosse Way. The right hand, going north-east, is Akeman Street which leaves the A.433 and heads off in its straight line to Coln St Aldwyns. The main road passes through the grey-stone line of the estate village with the unlikely name of Barnsley. The traffic thunders through, especially in Cirencester's morning and evening rush-hours, but Barnsley is to be visited in spring and summer when the gardens of Barnsley House are open. They have been created with great skill and loving care – the Cotswolds are full of fine English gardens and this is one of the most distinctive of them. Its showpiece is the long and spectacular Laburnum Walk, a vivid yellow tunnel cascading down, alluring, alarming, but there are greater and more subtle beauties here, and some inspired planting has matured magnificently.

Alas, the road from Cirencester to Fairford doesn't have a name. It's the dull old A.417 but it passes through the Ampneys – which are worth leaving it for. You come first to Ampney Crucis, with its church and

The Orpheus mosaic in the Corinium Museum

Cottages and the church in Barnsley

group of houses reached over a small bridge crossing Ampney Brook. In the churchyard is one of the few complete village crosses left – the Puritans broke the heads off most of them – with carved panels on all four sides.

Ampney St Peter is pleasing, very genteel, very peaceful; but the best of the Ampneys is the strange, isolated little church of Ampney St Mary, left high and dry in the middle of a field, at the end of a track that leads from the main road. Its village disappeared in the years of the Black Death, and St Mary's was abandoned – and became known as the ivy church, because ivy covered it when it was left empty and derelict for many years.

It has long grass in the graveyard, and some wonderful tombs covered in moss and grey-green lichen, leaning this way and that, but although it has been rescued from total neglect, it still has a strange, slightly

sad air. Inside, there are some traces of wall paintings – nothing like as good as many others in the Cotswolds – and on the wall outside, a carved tympanum over a Norman doorway, rather blurred and indistinct. It isn't really for individual relics or treasures that it's worth making a special pilgrimage to Ampney St Mary's; I like it because I always like slightly odd and lonely places, because it has melancholy echoes of the past, and of all the poor people who once throve and worshipped there, swept away by a cruel disease, and leaving behind, apart from a few tombstones, so little trace of lives lived, work done, families raised, joys and sorrows.

Now you stand in the graveyard, and the wind blows and stirs the grasses but disturbs nothing else,

The church and graveyard of Ampney St Mary

and the world dashes by on the road a hundred yards away, and there is only this small stone church to serve as a monument and a reminder.

Many a good English hymn has a tune named by its composer after a village, a town, a city, and one I am very fond of, *Come Down, O Love Divine*, was called by Vaughan Williams after the name of his birthplace – Down Ampney. Together with Elgar and Britten, Vaughan Williams is the composer I love best, his music speaks to me of the spirit of the English countryside, reminds me of it, evokes it, as nothing else can. So it was with some emotion that I set out to visit the village of his birth.

It lies a few miles south of the rest of the Ampneys, which form a close group of three, and equidistant from Fairford. And it was so unlike anything I might have been expecting that, in the end, my pilgrimage became more of a joke against my sentimental imaginings.

Down Ampney is a large, long and rather shapeless village, full of a startling variety of new houses, though there are some old cottages remaining. At the far end are the church and the fifteenth-century manor house, slightly stranded together. Down Ampney has grown because of the presence of the nearby airfield at Fairford (from which the Concorde flew on its early trials). This may be the birthplace of a great composer, then, but what you notice once inside the church is that it is dedicated to the Royal Air Force, and to the memory of the airmen of the Second World War. There is a full visitors' book in which ex-servicemen leave names, addresses, details of their squadrons and war service, together with comradely messages.

I have written tenderly of the ancient gravestones in many a Cotswold village church and, happily, the worst excesses of the modern monumental stonemasons have rarely been allowed to flourish in the region. The churchyard at Down Ampney, however, is a startling exception. It is a riot of engraved stone hearts, open stone books, and grieving cherubs. They are hideous, of course they are, and hideously out of place, though restraint itself by comparison with similar effigies in the cemeteries of Italy or France – and perhaps they had better be here than elsewhere in the Cotswolds. I began by being appalled at the sight of them, and by scoffing; and stayed to be corrected and to weep. For the emotion and the grief that inspired these monuments is no less keen, poignant or genuine than that exposed to the passer-by on more ancient or elegant gravestones, or those which to some will seem more artistically tasteful. For what is good taste in the face of human suffering?

Off the spoke of the wheel that points due west from Cirencester, in the direction of Stroud, lies the village of Coates – but just outside, take the sign that reads not 'Coates village' but 'Coates church'. On either side of the church there are two typical, handsome Cotswold houses, set behind high hedges and at the end of gravelled drives. They make as satisfactory a grouping as you might find.

It's difficult to say exactly why some churches feel good, and others depress. It has nothing really to do with whether or not they have fine Norman archways, well-preserved wall paintings, rare stone carvings or precious relics of medieval tiling. It has to do with the air of being well-used, still loved and cared for, with a congregation who worship and use the building as a focus of church life, too. It is people who give life to a church – or who do not.

St Matthew's Church at Coates has a good feeling. It is looked after and polished, and things happen here – that much is clear. When I was last there, it was summed up for me by the drawings and poems the Sunday School children had done, about the gargoyles on the outside of the church, and which were on display beside the door. They were all good – quirky, funny, direct, fresh, but one, by Ian Burdock, pleased me most of all.

The Church Cat
Have you seen the church cat,
All high up in the tower of the church?
Alone is he, white all over
But a happy cat.
As you pass by, listen for a purr.
How long has he been there?
Do you feel you're being watched?
Is he looking down on us?
Does he keep the church safe from mice?
He is not soft and furry
But cold as stone.
Was he a pet of the stone faces in the church?
Maybe you are happy to be watched.
Look up and see him looking down at you
For he is our church cat.

Go into the churchyard, and look up to see the gargoyles. Then if you go through the gate at the back of the churchyard which leads onto a field path, you can take a walk of half a mile or so, and find one end of a curious piece of Cotswold history. The footpath leads over several fields until you reach the railway. Being wary of trains, you cross the track and a little way ahead, at the bottom of a very steep bank, lies the entrance to the tunnel of the Thames and Severn Canal, through which a great many freight-carrying barges once passed until the canal was overtaken by the railway and it became derelict. Beside the tunnel is a pub, Tunnel House.

And the other end of this piece of history, the other end of the tunnel, is a couple of miles away. You could walk there and it's easy by road – but you can't use the canal or its tunnel any more. Either way, you finish up close to one of my most favourite of all Cotswold villages, but one which is in many ways quite untypical – Sapperton. Beside the bridge at this end is the Daneway Inn, both pubs built to serve thirsty bargees.

The village of Sapperton perches high above the valley of the young River Frome, and here there is a most curious church. It was mainly rebuilt in the eighteenth century, severe and classical and cold, with extraordinary wooden pews whose every end is carved with strange, naked Eastern figures which don't look

St Matthew, Coates, on a stormy December morning

as if they belong in a Christian church – and indeed do not, for they came from Sapperton House when it was demolished in about 1730.

But, in spite of its oddness and its ornate ugly classical monuments, I warmed to St Kenelm's Church, Sapperton, for the same reason as I so like St Matthew's, Coates. It is lived in, well-used, alive – and the Sunday School is much in evidence. There was a dancing frieze, all about the miracles of Jesus – including an invitation to the marriage feast at Caana, with the careful addition of – R.S.V.P.

Outside, walk down beside the church and through a gate, into a steeply sloping field. Opposite rises the thickly-wooded slope of the other side of this beautiful valley. In spring, the birdsong is incredible; in autumn, the trees are all the colours of gold, and in winter, in the snow, the bare bones of the landscape are revealed, whilst at the bottom of the ravine, the air is achingly cold. Sapperton stands high, perched on the hill, with some quite beautiful stone houses all dotted around. It feels exhilarating, it looks exactly right in its setting, it is very quiet.

I left the village and walked down the steep lane, over the bridge, and sat in the sun in the window of the Daneway Inn. Outside, the air sparkled, the sunlight came sifting through the trees, and inside the little, dark-wood bar, you could hear the clock tick. A Saturday morning in the Cotswolds, and no one else in the world. An hour later, it would be filled to overflowing with loud weekenders, smart cars.

Walk up through the woods and out onto the open ridge – and again, there will probably be no one. That's the way it is, in the Cotswolds.

Sapperton. (Opposite) *View across the village roofs to the church and* (below) *looking across to Daneway.* (Overleaf) *View down the Frome Valley*

9. The Duntisbourne Valley

Some places in the Cotswolds seem so familiar you feel as if you've known about them forever, just as you've known Stratford-upon-Avon, or Blackpool, or Clovelly, even though you may never actually have been to them. You know them from picture post-cards and tea trays and Home-made Clotted Cream Toffee tins but their faces have grown as familiar as the faces of Royalty, so that when you do finally arrive in Bourton-on-the-Water or Bibury or Broadway, you have a curious sense of unreality, almost as though you are stepping onto a film-set, or into one of those places you dream about and imagine you must have invented, only to find them coming true.

But there are other places you may find all for yourself, quietly one out-of-season day, and they reveal their overall charm, as well as their incidental glories, bit by bit, and you have all the pride of the early discoverers. Only later, it may come as something of a disappointment to learn that other people know the place, that it has been extensively written about, and all its beauties were photographed long ago.

Perhaps it doesn't really matter, but what I *have* learned is that the best way to safeguard your chances of becoming a discoverer is to travel with a map only – preferably an Ordnance Survey map – and, although I say it against myself, never with any sort of gazetteer or guide-book.

Yes, of course it is more efficient to have the latter: that way you will be sure to see everything someone else has told you is worth seeing and so avoid wasting time on the uninteresting or unimportant. If time matters at all, that is, but it shouldn't. Best leave time behind somewhere; and if you have only a day or a weekend to spare, simply be prepared to see less and to cover less ground, but to enjoy the surprise of coming upon things by accident, and the satisfaction of having made the journey of discovery by yourself.

I always feel depressed at the sight of tourist coach after coach after coach making the well-trodden round of the well-known sights, and at the glazed, and often quite uninterested eyes in the faces that peer from the tinted windows; no excitement, no voyage of dis-

Duntisbourne Leer at dawn; (right) *the interior of St John, Elkstone*

*Christ in Majesty, the tympanum over the south door
at Elkstone church*

covery there, nor any chance of getting lost, or of having even the smallest adventure, only the satisfaction of ticking off names on a printed list.

If that sounds like a superior sneer, it is not meant to: I am only sorry that the visitors have missed so much in trying to accomplish too much in a couple of days.

All of which is by way of preamble to some of the villages of the Duntisbourne valley which I discovered one weekend in bleakest January and returned to six months later, newly conscious of their fame and, in terms of churches, their importance. For within ten miles or so are some of the rarest and most remarkable examples of English small-church architecture in the country and some of the most gravely beautiful stone-

work. All of which dawned upon me gradually, hour by hour, as I explored.

It was one of the coldest weekends of the year, iron-cold, too cold by far for snow and, in any case, there were no snow clouds in the sky. The sun shone but there was no warmth in it, and in the shadow of all the hedges and trees and under the dry-stone walls and down deep in every ditch, the ground stayed white with a thick frost, and all the grasses stiff. It was not surprising that the Cotswolds were half empty, that for mile after mile on the back lanes and by-roads, there was no other car.

I had driven across country from Stratford-upon-Avon, and on the top roads you could see for miles. The air was brilliantly clear, and the high Cotswold places like Condicote and Snowshill, and the wide fields above the Guitings, seemed as remote and lonely and exposed to the cold winds and weather as many a village on the Yorkshire moors.

I was making, in an odd, diagonal sort of way, first for Cirencester and then for Tetbury – which is how, via roads and a route no one with half a sense of direction would have taken, I found myself beside a signpost pointing me to Elkstone. And remembering that someone I knew slightly lived there and had spoken warmly of it, I drove down the lane that led to the church – about which I knew nothing.

It looked good enough, with a pleasing tower, but I saw nothing at once remarkable, and certainly no hint of the rare beauty I was to find within. Only a handsome-looking stone house, glimpsed down a long drive, and many trees surrounding the graveyard, bare apart from the gloomy firs and yews.

I went into the graveyard which sloped away from me. To one side, another, more modest stone house, with its ground floor back windows at eye level with the grass and the graves. I liked that, and the table-top tombs carved with strangely old-faced cherubs, and sinister skull-and-crossbones.

And then I saw the doorway and the tympanum, and began to realise that Elkstone was indeed special: anywhere with a good carved stone tympanum will earn a place in my heart, and this at the church of St John, Elkstone, over the south door, is one of the best I have ever seen. It shows Christ in Majesty, seated under the hand of God, and in a perfect half-hoop surrounding it are beakheads, odd but friendly, not grotesque.

Inside, the church was as cold as the grave, the sort of cold that made you gasp, and when you gasped the

The evening road home

cold air made your chest hurt. It was the first of many cold churches that bitter weekend. After a while, I got used to them. No, of course, they can't keep every country church in England in a glow of central heating and who would want it, even if they could? Only it is perhaps sad that flesh and blood could not have borne to linger there, and certainly not for long enough to kneel and pray.

Elkstone is a little church and comparatively un-cluttered, and its pride and glory is its chancel: it is small, and very early. The stone arches are carved with careful zig-zags, and the low roof is vaulted so that your eye is led gently inwards, through each arch, to the heart. There, the light is golden as if concealed lamps were permanently lit on either side – in fact, the effect comes from the coloured glass in the side windows, out of sight. Straight ahead, in the very narrow centre window, is a Virgin and Child in stained glass of a deep, deep ultramarine blue.

I am not at all sure that I like it. It is modern but not modern enough, not ugly but just not good enough either for this austerely beautiful setting. I should like to see clear glass that lets in the daylight and the moonlight, or else a window by John Piper.

On that bleak mid-winter day, the road took me a mile or so west, and then south down the Duntis-bourne valley to villages whose names on the map I liked the sound of but of which I had never before heard: Duntisbourne Abbots, Duntisbourne Leer, Duntisbourne Rouse, Daglingworth.

By the time I reached Cirencester it was almost dark, it had not lifted above freezing all day, and I had not seen a single other human being in my pilgrimage. Each village, each church, was completely deserted, silent and still, though there began to be lamps lit in windows as the afternoon drew in, and I did not once feel uneasy or alone.

Duntisbourne Abbots village

But it was as if I had discovered lost villages that had been buried in time.

The churchyard of St Peter, Duntisbourne Abbots

The next time I came to Elkstone, six months later, it was a hot, balmy afternoon of high summer, and the trees that fringe the graveyard were full-skirted and thickly green. Inside, a small boy was practising on a violin to piano accompaniment, and the stone walls rang with his music, and beyond the open doorway the birds vied with him, and all their notes flew up to heaven together.

Coming next to the villages of the Duntisbourne valley, and now knowing them to be famous after all, I expected to find them over-run with cars and visitors, as well as full of the people who live there. They were not. On a golden summer Saturday afternoon, the Duntisbournes, and their churches, were as quiet as ever.

A few people worked in their gardens. There were recent names in the visitors' books in all the churches and the addresses showed how far they came to see these places they must have read about: from Hawaii, and Kansas, and Christchurch, New Zealand, and Bishop Auckland, County Durham. But always, by the time I got there, the others had flown on ahead or home again, and I was quite alone, sitting on benches in the churchyards, reading the names on the graves, re-discovering what I had first come upon with such delight the previous winter.

And the best churchyard for sitting in is that of the northernmost village of Duntisbourne Abbots, which has a nicely placed bench from which you can enjoy not the sight of the church itself, for you have your back to it, but the rolling, rambling rectangular churchyard, around which are set some of the most pleasing small houses in the Cotswolds. Immediately opposite the bench is one cottage with the most wonderful tiled roof and the long slope of one side of it runs sheer down until it meets the grass of the graveyard.

Up the church path, leading from the curious revolving lych-gate, old gravestones are ranged on either side, stiffly upright as a wedding guard of honour. I very often like the outsides of churches a great deal better than the insides.

(Below) *Duntisbourne Abbots seen from Duntisbourne Leer;* (right) *the ford and raised walkway*

The village of Duntisbourne Abbots slopes steeply uphill. Stand at the lych-gate of the church and look down to the roofs of cottages and barns and little old stone privies at the bottom of gardens, and around, to the grey stone houses. There are no straight lines, yet everything is orderly. It is a snug village, looking in upon itself. Someone closes a door on one side of the sloping green, and the sound echoes sharply across to the other. A path takes you down to the bottom lane, and then if you look up and ahead, you see the green slopes of the fields beyond, rising up between the houses and the gaps in the trees.

Further along is a small ford and the brook slips over flat stones and beside a narrow raised walkway. Cross it, and up and out – the village in the valley. Duntisbourne Abbots is one of the most peaceful, hidden villages in all the Cotswolds.

And the next village going south, Duntisbourne Leer, is one of the most picture-book pretty. It ought to be spoiled. It is entirely photogenic and doubtless much photographed, yet it remains genuine, unself-conscious, a real place. It is also very small, scarcely more than a hamlet.

On the almost too-perfect June day, I stopped the car a yard or two away from the ford that runs across the road and through which you have to splash to get out of the village at all. When the engine was still, there was only the sound of doves and pigeons coo-coo-cooing from dozens of square holes let into the stone walls of two of the houses, the most drowsy sound of high summer. It was very hot. I went and stood in the stream and let it trickle over my welling-ton boots, and then sloshed gently about a bit, because that, after all, is what you should do in streams and fords. Behind me, in the farmyard, ducks lay asleep, surrounded by egg-yolk yellow babies, puffs of feathers on the gravel, and a sheepdog dozed, but one eye was open and altogether aware of me.

The garden by the brook in Duntisbourne Leer

The ford at Duntisbourne Leer and resident ducks

Beside the brook which runs away between deep banks, the sort of cottage garden all cottage gardens should be like, with bean wigwams and sweet-pea canes, and rows of blue blue delphiniums, and sweet williams, all mixed up with lines of feathery-headed carrots, fresh green onions and leafy potatoes, while frilly clove pinks edged the lettuce beds. There was a bee-hive in a corner. And everywhere, the peonies were full out, at their blowsy, wanton best; boudoir pink, paper white and lipstick red, and when I leaned over a stone wall, their smell was indescribably sweet.

I tried to imagine what it would be like at Duntis-bourne Leer on a dank day in November, when everything dripped and the gardens were bare and the grey of the sky met the grey of the stone and there was no light in the rooms of the cottages. Places that lie at the bottom of river valleys can be claustrophobic and damp and drear and, perhaps, in quiet Duntisbourne Leer, it is so. I like to live high, nearer to the sky and the tree tops; but on a good day, to be cool and shady for a while beside the trickling water at Duntisbourne Leer is an excellent thing.

You could very satisfactorily become a collector of

The Saxon church of St Michael at Duntisbourne Rouse with (above) *the gate and grassy approach to it*

things in the Cotswold churches – wall paintings, Norman arches, carved fonts, table-top tombs. I have already mentioned my penchant for tympanums, and Lion and Unicorn boards, but I have also grown especially fond of plain wooden box pews, and saddle-back towers. When I find the two together in one utterly unspoilt place, in a church which retains Saxon features, has had no additions since the seventeenth century, and no restorations, I feel a particular pleasure. And the lovely church dedicated to St Michael at Duntisbourne Rouse has a lot more, too.

Its setting is one of the most perfect in the whole Cotswolds. It stands high up, and overlooks the steep slope that runs down to the Duntisbourne Brook and then up again on the far side, so that if you stand on the edge of the graveyard, you feel you might fly across like an angel, there is such a sense of lightness and airy space.

From the gate, the church path leads down, very straight between neat hedges, and instead of being of gravel or stone, it is grass – so that your foot falls softly, and nothing disturbs the quiet save the birds.

A flower and vegetable garden in Daglingworth

St Michael's saddle-back tower is very small, its nave is Saxon and unadorned, the box pews are lovely. The first time I went there was in that bitter cold, and it was growing dark. This time the sun shone, and I lingered among the graves and found a very fresh one, unusual in an old churchyard where few are now buried. Whoever lay there, his new mound still covered in flowers, must rest quiet in his grave in that most beautiful spot. I read some of the cards on the sprays and wreaths. Why does one do that? Why not? They were touching beyond bearing, they spoke of love and grief and immortality. I shall never forget them.

No one else was about. The church is one of a group of parishes so that there are infrequent services, but St Michael's is cared for, it does not feel neglected or unused.

I thought how full the Cotswold villages are of ordinary, everyday human life, and of the important things that happen to people, as they have been happening for hundreds of years; I thought of the

THE DUNTISBOURNE VALLEY [151]

deaths and the burials, the graves and the memorials, and the births and the christenings in all those solemn stone fonts. And the marriages and the marriage feasts, and how everything happens at random, together, the joys and the sorrows weaving in and out of one another.

I left St Michael's at Duntisbourne Rouse reflecting on the grave I had just seen and what it meant, and on all the other graves in all the other churchyards, the stones that marked the end of so many brief lives. And drove into Daglingworth, the last village in the Duntisbourne valley, to see a wedding feast at the village hall. The church was all pink and white and blooming, with posies and ribbons on the end of every row of pews, and fresh confetti sinking into the clumps of grass beside the gate.

Daglingworth's church has much that is Saxon about it, too; there is something so austere, so elemental and calm about that period's architecture. It appeals to me greatly now, far more than the ornate and the over-decorated.

Because I hadn't read up about the Church of the Holy Rood at Daglingworth before I went there the first time, I came upon its chief treasures all unprepared – and I'm glad I did. There are three Saxon stone sculptures and they took my breath away, they are so utterly simple, and moving. There is St Peter with his keys, a Christ in glory, and a Crucifixion. It is the sort of Crucifixion which makes you believe that that terrible thing really happened to a real man. There's nothing symbolic about it, for all its lack of elaborate detail; it is primitive and stark, the figure small and a little like a man drawn by a child. And yet, of course, it *is* symbolic, it bears a weight of meaning. On either side of the cross stand the two Roman soldiers, one carrying the spear and the other the sponge and the pot of vinegar. They are small, stubby figures, their faces shadowy, with scarcely any features marked. But they are indubitably real men, too.

I'd travelled down the Duntisbourne valley unaware of what I was to find; and as I went from place to place, I became more and more serious, more and more reflective. The spirit abroad in these small churches and their silent villages has that effect. You retreat into yourself here, become contemplative, and you leave feeling all set to rights – restored.

Saxon carving of St Peter with his keys in the Church of the Holy Rood, Daglingworth

10. The Churn Valley

I have never seen a ghost. I know plenty of people who know other people who have, of course, we all do – the ghost always seems to be at several removes! I'm not sure whether I really believe in them or not.

But I am obliged to believe in haunted places because I have occasionally experienced them and always quite unexpectedly. Certain houses, villages, odd corners of the countryside, suddenly make me feel unbearably uneasy, shivery, anxious to be gone. Sometimes, the reason why is obvious enough – the houses are old and dark with creaking floorboards and secret rooms, tucked away passages leading in and out of one another without warning so that you easily become lost, and anyone coming, soft-footed, around a corner can startle you horribly. Often, of course, these places have a bloody and unhappy history. I don't understand why violent events and the extremes of past emotion – terror, dread, anguish – seem to leave an everlasting aura, but they often do. And it's rarely when I've been told that a place is haunted that I feel a frisson for myself – rather the contrary – the more famous the ghost, the less likely am I to be troubled!

There are plenty of ghosts in the Cotswolds; go to the folklore section in the public libraries in Cheltenham or Cirencester, and you can find a nice collection of hooded monks, and anguished nuns who wring their hands, of phantom coaches that charge over crossroads and men in eighteenth-century riding-dress who pace the lanes at midnight! There are witches, too, and a

Hampnett, seen from Northleach church tower

few stories of more sinister happenings than harmless hauntings. It isn't surprising – the area is full of pre-history and recent history: there are long barrows full of bones and the shades of Roman armies, innumerable isolated farms and dark old manor houses, and every graveyard tells a story.

Often enough I have had a sense of the past pressing in upon me, imagined people long dead and places as they once were. When walking and thinking and exploring in the Cotswolds, once or twice only I have come upon a place I have not liked because, for some reason difficult to explain at the time, it has made me feel chill and a little afraid or, worse, choked and claustrophobic. Occasionally, I have looked up the name and learned of a legend which might, if I were superstitious, have made me nod my head wisely. But I am not superstitious. On the whole, I incline towards the mundane, if obscure, explanation for my state of mind and feeling.

No, I don't think I *do* believe in ghosts.

But I did have a very unpleasant morning in one corner of the Cotswolds. And I do not have any *entirely* satisfactory explanation for all my feelings – I only know that I was heartily glad to get away. I wasn't alone, either, it was a shared experience of unease. The Cotswolds showed not a hideous but a blank face, featureless and dead, and the past and the present – and perhaps even the future – felt unfriendly. Make of it what you will.

It all began with the weather. It was the end of June, and June had been universally wet so that the countryside was lush green and everywhere overgrown, the hedges thick, the ditches high; the freshness and delicacy of spring were long gone, and we had had none of the clear blue sky and hot sunshine of a good summer.

On this particular Saturday morning, it was not actually raining, but the clouds were low and heavy-bellied, and a mist hung down and dampened the face and hair like clinging cobwebs. Everything was still, there was not a hint of a breeze. And it was warm – too warm; a dozen words applied to the weather – close, muggy, humid, steamy, swampy, clammy. The Cotswolds were oddly quiet for the time of year, and everywhere and everyone looked vaguely dispirited.

We were making for the villages of the Churn valley, and thence to Cirencester but, coming from farther north, had decided to fill in a piece of the country that lies at the top of the triangle formed by the two Roman roads that run into Cirencester – the Ermine Way (A.417) from Gloucester and the Fosse Way (A.429) from Stow, and the A.436 and A.40 that is the line across the triangle top.

I had planned to visit Chedworth again for its Roman villa, and Rendcomb which lies high at the head of the Churn valley, and to see several unfamiliar villages sparsely scattered a few miles further north.

The first of these was Hampnett from where, I had read, one would have a fine view of the tower of Northleach church rising out of the surrounding meadows. But we couldn't see that far because of the mist so we turned our attention to the church. It is Norman, and good enough from the outside. I looked it up in a book and read that in the 1870s the chancel and sanctuary were 'decorated' by the vicar in order to recreate the look of the church in medieval times.

I wasn't sure if I liked the sound of that. We went inside. I liked the look of it a good deal less. If this is really what medieval churches were like, with russet-coloured stencilling all over the plain Cotswold stone, I'm glad nothing much of the work has survived. Hampnett has been made hideous, gaudy and Byzantine. I wanted to scrape it all off. And I see that the villagers once actually opened a fund to pay for the removal of the paintings – alas, not enough money was raised and now I learn that the attempt to recreate medieval church decoration is once more fully ap-

The gaudy interior of St George, Hampnett

preciated and the wretched stuff is to be everlastingly preserved.

Feeling that I was obviously out of tune with the times, I came rather crossly out of the church at Hampnett into eerie, oppressive, misty quiet. The fields stretched all around, unfenced and bleak-looking; now and then a sheep bleated. There were one or two neglected-looking barns and farm buildings and not a living soul. I began to feel uneasy. We walked a little way, saw some pretty cottages set below us, near willow trees and a stream. Still no sign of people. A deserted village.

Then the cries came. Shrieks – raucous, harsh and, for a moment, quite unidentifiable, but when we looked towards the trees from which the sound came, we saw flashes of gold and scarlet – and then the huge wings of great, jazzy-bright macaws. The birds were rising up from a cage and flitting about among the top branches of a clump of trees and back again. They looked exotic, odd, and totally incongruous; gaudy, tropical things in a subdued English country setting. And their cries were most unpleasantly eerie.

We left Hampnett rather quickly. The countryside

we drove through was some of the dullest and least interesting I had so far encountered in the Cotswolds and, like the village we had left, it was quite deserted – we passed no other car, no rider, no farmer in any field. It is not splendidly bleak up here as it is, say, up at Condicote or Snowshill, or on the high exposed ridge of road running towards Cheltenham from the north – it is rather featureless and dead. On this particular lowering, grey day, the corn was high and there was a lot of it, and cornfields are, except when the sun and shadow go rippling prettily over them, visually very uninteresting. All around the cornfields, there were dark woods of too many conifers, giving that uniform, dark-green dead look to the countryside that is only one of the things wrong with conifer plantations. And striding across the whole landscape, the pylons, those hideous science-fictional scarecrows, unforgivable blots on many an English landscape.

We were beginning to feel oppressed – by the weather that closed us in, by the cornfields and conifers and pylons and the total lack of any sign of humanity. We drove on, after dithering at a crossroads, uphill through the trees, and the dark, dank woods pressed in on either side.

'I don't think I like this,' I said.

We agreed that we would find a signpost that pointed us towards a village, or at least the main road, and get back to civilisation and a pub for lunch.

Easier said than done. We had to pull into the ditch close to the trees to let a tractor go by on the narrow road, and the driver, hunched up, and with his shoulders covered in old sacking, did not acknowledge us – did not, indeed, seem aware of our existence, only stared dully through us, and straight ahead.

'Perhaps he doesn't exist,' I said jokily, 'perhaps he's a ghostly tractor driver.'

Not funny.

I began to feel more uneasy. We were in an area which had once been heavily occupied by the Roman armies; all around here, remains of camps and villas have been found and I began to wonder about violent battles, or unhappy Roman soldiers going mad or committing suicide in the bleak, grey Cotswold winter countryside. No. Whatever gloomy spirit was abroad, it was not that. I felt the Roman soldiers were quite unfrightening in any ghostly sense. So empty was the landscape as we drove on, desperately searching for a signpost and a way out, that the brilliant sight of the Roman army on the march might, however ghostly, have been a welcome relief.

We took several false turnings down lanes that petered out into cart tracks, and came upon too many deserted, dilapidated, boarded-up barns and buildings.

And then we were out of the woods, on the top, so

high now that the low clouds hung even lower, the mist clung even closer, and when we opened the car windows, all was still, still, and the air steamy-warm. And up here, the roads all ran together into one another, and into a sort of crazy, wide-open space, like the runways of a disued airfield. At last, a signpost – but the arm had been snapped off. We came upon another like that, and another, then a whole cluster of four, and every one snapped off, like broken teeth. We were lost, we had no idea how to find a way out, and now we felt more than uneasy, haunted, not by some sad Cotswold ghost of the past, but by some awful event in the future. I've never had any feeling quite like it before.

Another signpost, a very small one, pointing down a gloomy looking, very narrow lane, between trees. 'Cheltenham'. I simply didn't believe it and we didn't feel like experimenting. And still there was no one else in sight.

Until we looked up from the map on our knees and straight down the gun barrel of a tank which had rolled up to us noiselessly out of the mist. It was covered in bits of hedge and twig and several soldiers in tin helmets and camouflage, and at any other time I would have giggled since they would have looked as silly as such soldiers playing soldiers always do. Not today. Today they only looked sinister, and stared through us impassively and then vanished into the mist and we would not have dared to ask them the way, for fear of . . .

Well, of what? Of what?

I don't know. I only know that we tossed dice and drove in the direction instinct and panic told us must, *must* lead to the main road; we drove very fast, and in complete silence. And on fence posts here and there stood dreadful hooded crows. We passed no one. The road went on for ever. If we had broken down anywhere up in those silent places, I should have gone berserk. These were the haunted Cotswolds, and we were afraid and when, quite suddenly, we hit the main road, we began to laugh hysterically and with relief.

At the pub in North Cerney we stopped because we were hungry, but more, because there were a lot of cars in the car park, and we needed plenty of normal, cheerful human company. And as we crossed to the door, the sun came out, parting the chilly mist, and suddenly it was a glorious, hot summer's day.

But I shall not go back into the haunted triangle again. We saw no ghosts, heard no phantom galloping hooves, there was no sense of past events, there were no creepy looking, old stone houses. It was a drear day, filled with a sense of oppression and our own fear.

Haunted places?

The rest of the day I remember so well perhaps because of the very contrast with the morning. For it was indeed a golden afternoon. The Cotswolds began to look as the homesick Englishman abroad remembers them, and as the transatlantic visitor imagines and hopes to find them. The stones of all the pretty little cottages and handsome manor houses were honey- and butter-coloured and the first flush of roses was appearing, Albertine and Frühlingsgold, Sanders White and Gloire de Dijon clambering up and cascading down. Cottage gardens glimpsed down passageways and through open gates and over walls were rich with lupins, peonies, geraniums, and bearded iris straight as swords, paper-white, Cambridge blue and deep, deep purple. And the air smelled of the mowing of a hundred lawns, and the Queen Anne's lace was waist-high along every verge.

By the time we had eaten and drunk and felt the shadows of the morning disperse, the sun was high and hot and the shady lane that leads up to All Saints Church, North Cerney, was welcome.

But even more welcome to me was the sight of the churchyard full of sheep. Because it was hot, they

The valley of the River Churn

were lying quietly, panting just a little for their heavy, knotted, shaggy coats had not yet been shorn. There were no more than fifteen of them, ewes with their rather large lambs, and I stood looking at them, and at the picture they composed, among the gravestones and the long grass and against the backdrop of the church, for a long time.

I was wondering why it is that I like sheep so much, what exactly it is about them that makes them so decorative; they are not intelligent, they do not, unless they are orphaned lambs, relate much to people, and their bleating, though it can echo plaintively through the imagination and stir all manner of associations, is really rather inane – yet I never tire of the noise, just as I never tire of looking at sheep. One of my pipe-dreams is to have the fields below my own house permanently full of them, and one of the chief joys of journeying through the Cotswolds is the sight of sheep everywhere – scattered at random like white confetti over hillsides, grazing among fruit trees in old orchards,

streaming across lanes and up tracks like some foaming white river, or just sitting in North Cerney churchyard. (They have electric fencing to keep them in, which is not particularly attractive but entirely necessary.)

The Cotswolds prospered on the backs of sheep. Those who graze the grasslands today are the heirs of a very long line. They look quite ordinary nowadays, just like sheep anywhere, but the original Cotswold sheep were much larger and were bred for the weight of their fleeces. You can see a few of the traditional long-necked breed in among other rare breeds of animal (Gloucester Old Spot pigs, for example) at the Cotswold Farm Park at Guiting Power.

In the Middle Ages, the whole air must have echoed all day long to the cries of the sheep, you could have counted them by the million. The church did well by sheep – all the abbeys in the area (and there were many) kept flocks, and so did the bishops. Northleach church and Chipping Campden church, and Fairford and Lechlade too, are still called the 'wool churches', built, or restored, or enlarged or decorated as they were by the merchants who became rich in the trade, and innumerable village churches had treasures restored or alterations and repairs carried out too. It was the wool merchants who built themselves such handsome stone houses, and the marvellous great barns for storing wool that still survive all over the area. It was the wool trade which made those villages conveniently situated at cross roads into small market towns for the sale of sheep, and then the towns flourished and expanded.

The Cotswolds prospered on the backs of sheep

Wool meant cloth, and so the Stroud valley filled and grew prosperous when the spinners and weavers, cloth workers and dyers settled there, close to good sources of water. For several hundred years, the Cotswolds meant sheep meant wool meant cloth meant prosperity. And the buildings that were built were built of the local stone, men quarried at their feet to raise roofs over their heads, as well as places of worship to their God. And the look of the sheep blends in with the look of the stone houses and churches and barns. One of the more important things about the Cotswolds as a whole is this indigenous visual harmony.

So that, standing in the churchyard at North Cerney,

among the peaceful sheep, the sense of the continuity of English history is very strong, even in me, and I don't reckon to have, at least in the abstract, a very strong historical sense. But it is the moments when the past and its people and their ordinary everyday lives seem to be part of the immediate present, to be alive and unchanged and interweaving with one's own life – those are important, those bring the centuries together and make nonsense of time and mortality.

The sight of one of the mighty churches is always awe-inspiring. I am always amazed that mere men, living in an age which did not have the benefits of modern machinery, could construct churches like those at Cirencester or Burford, but I don't feel close to them, cannot imagine them; the effect of such lofty grandeur is to distance me. But by the small, almost domestic details of more modest buildings, I am often brought sharply up against the reality of past lives.

Sheep in the churchyard of All Saints, North Cerney

Before you go into All Saints at North Cerney, look at the fourteenth-century porch. Look at the tiles on its pitched roof. They make a perfect pattern, and the individual tiles are mossy and blotched by time and the weather, and each one is a very slightly different shade from its neighbour, yet they all blend perfectly together. Now go under the porch, and look up. The tiles lie neatly one upon one, like a pack of cards pulled out from the top, and in between are the wooden pegs that secure them on. It is not only delightful, even and satisfying to look at – it makes me picture the workman who patiently, quietly, laid them there and made the porch what it was. There are tile roofs like it all over the Cotswolds, just as there are miles of dry-stone walls, intricately, beautifully laid, and every time I see one, I marvel at the skills of so many anonymous men.

There is much else to enjoy in North Cerney: a beautiful wine-glass pulpit, a squint passage and, on the outside south wall, some curious, primitive scratch markings, of a manticore – a human-headed guard-dog – and a leopard.

The interior of the porch of All Saints; (right) *a typical Cotswold drystone wall;* (below) *a network of Cotswold walls near Chedworth Lanes*

The font at St Peter, Rendcomb

We sat on a gravestone in the sun, and felt very contented among the bleating sheep, and I was told the story of someone who was married here, and when she came for her wedding rehearsal was assured that, of course, on the day itself, the sheep would have been removed from the churchyard. Only she protested at once, that certainly not, the sheep were to be there, she wanted to be married with the sheep all around the church and their cries floating in through the door.

And so she was.

From North Cerney, we first went on along the Churn road a few miles, to Rendcomb, perched above the valley – and there is one of those glorious bits of complete incongruity which lend such eccentric charm to England for it would be woe indeed if everywhere looked dully in period and in keeping, like one of those film sets where they keep ostentatiously showing you how authentic the cigarette packets are and not a wrong note is struck and the researchers are to be congratulated and it is all very dull and oddly unreal.

Rendcomb is oddly unreal, too, and I liked it a lot because it is so unlikely. St Peter's Church is pretty traditional, another of the wool churches, donated by Sir Edmund Tame, a rich wool merchant whose father had rebuilt the magnificent church at Fairford. It has one of the best fonts in the region, carved with twelve arcades and the figures of eleven apostles (with the niche for Judas left empty) – worth coming a long distance to see.

But it's not the church that dominates the village, it is Rendcomb College – a boys' public school – and the buildings are extraordinary, designed in the 1860s by

Philip Hardwick in the Italianate style. The stables, topped by a tall tower, look as if they are part of some French military equestrian academy – there are buildings very like them at Saumur, on the Loire.

On that sunny June afternoon, we strolled about, watching a vigorous tennis match, and admiring and being amused by these buildings, set down in the middle of a lush, green, utterly Cotswold valley. And then we walked through the wide stable yard – part of the school – towards an archway. Beyond it, at our feet, lay the most gloriously English sight.

The Cotswold hills, meadows full of buttercups, and grassy green slopes surrounded us in a beautiful bowl under the sky, and there, in the middle of it all, was the cricket field with a match in progress. We sat on a step and watched, and I could have stayed forever and been utterly content, since one version of paradise for me is a cricket match on a perfectly situated ground on a June day of glorious sunshine in the heart of England. It was a scene straight out of *England, Their England*, or Hugh de Selincourt's immortal novel *The Cricket Match*, the figures in their immaculate flannels moving so gracefully in the dance that is cricket, the stroke of leather on willow, the occasional cry and, from the opposite hillside, the bleating of sheep – oh, the scene contained every cliché in the book, and it was unforgettable.

From Rendcomb, everyone's vision of forever England under the summer sun, we returned, following the line of the River Churn, and at North Cerney took off across country towards the hamlet of Bagendon which lies in a dip between two hills, beside a brook. And of all the places that ought to be haunted, it is this apparently insignificant little cluster of Saxon church, mill and mill house, barns, farm and a few cottages. It is as quiet a place as any you will find in the Cotswolds. Hard to believe that in the first century, invaders of Britain known as the Dobunni established their capital here. They built a defensive ditch, enclosed two hun-

The entrance to the stables, Rendcomb College

dred acres, smelted metal and manufactured metal goods, and lived a comparatively civilised life, too, from the evidence archaeologists have unearthed around Bagendon – much of which can now be seen in the Corinium Museum at Cirencester. Coins were minted here, glass and great stone jars of wine were imported from the Continent, and though their huts were made of wattle, they had stone floors and proper doors latched by iron latches. It must have been a busy place, full of industrious and important people.

And then the Romans came and founded Corinium – Cirencester – as their second city. The centre of civilisation had moved, and the smiths and cattle merchants of the Dobunni gravitated towards it. Bagendon was deserted.

I walked a little way up a shady lane, and looked down on the hamlet absolutely quiet in the afternoon sun. All around, placidly grazing cows and silently growing corn. No ghosts at all. The Dobunni may have buried their dead here, but they lie quite peacefully in their common graves.

The little church of St Margaret has a small saddleback tower, and there are ducks in the brook that runs from the mill house, and the steep lanes that lead out of Bagendon are leafy and secluded. And I could happily have sat all day in the sun, and dabbled my feet in the cool, still waters.

While I was in Bagendon, I began to wonder about the lives not of the ancient tribe of the Dobunni, but of those who came much later, the genteel families who inhabited all the manor houses and rectories of the Cotswolds in the eighteenth and nineteenth centuries, when life was still in some ways medieval, and great happenings abroad did not touch at all upon those who spent their quiet days within the same small rural area. There were carriages then, for the rich, and pony traps, and horses to ride, but travel was still a great business; you did not undertake it without an upheaval, and it cannot ever have been particularly comfortable. So, for much of the time, people stayed where they were, and if they wanted to pay visits, as often as not they walked – over poor or non-existent roads, and along muddy lanes and through the long grass of fields and parks, the women in long skirts. And the poor, of course, always walked and many of them never left their own village in their whole lives.

I thought of long, long winter days, of cold and grey

The tiny village of Bagendon with St Margaret's church

and wet, in these silent hamlets at the bottom of the river valleys, when it was dark by four o'clock and there were only candles for illumination and cards and embroidery and improving books to pass the time. The stone manor houses would have been draughty and deathly cold, and the cottages of the poor dirty and smoke-filled and overcrowded, with children, the old and the animals all mewed up together.

How isolated and drear life in the Cotswolds must have seemed then, and how precious days like the one I now enjoyed, when the air was sweet with flowers and birdsong and bees, and the evenings were warm as the shadows lengthened.

How precious the visual treasures of the village churches must have been, too, for those who could not read, and for the young and the reluctant who were obliged to sit through several services every Sunday. What a delight then to have lived at Baunton, the last village in the Churn valley, before both road and river reach Cirencester. For the Norman church of St Mary Magdalene there has the most strikingly beautiful and immaculately preserved medieval wall painting I have ever seen. So often, the fragments of wall painting that survive, or have been uncovered, are disappointingly, tantalisingly sketchy – pale russet or blue marks fading into a crumbling background; here a devil, there an angel, parts of a crucifixion, dim to decipher.

But the painting of St Christopher at Baunton looks as startling and fresh as if it had been completed by the children of the village school, just the previous week. It takes up a great sweep of the wall immediately facing you as you enter, and the composition is so primitive and so curiously modern-looking, it appeals at once to the twentieth-century eye. And the colours are still vivid and vibrant which is unusual, too.

A great St Christopher is striding out across the

(Opposite) *14th-century wall-painting in Baunton church*

countryside in which, behind him, lie a windmill, two churches, some sketchy houses, a small person sitting on a bank all dressed in white, and a shaggy pony. The water of the stream swirls about the saint's feet, and it is this that is on eye level, so that you can go close up to the fish and the ships and the mermaid with her mirror and peer deep into the blue-green depths. And the Christ-child sits on St Christopher's red-cloaked shoulders.

To have had that to enjoy must have made the longest sermon tolerable – it probably still does.

The village of Baunton was quiet enough, but there was a lady polishing the church brass who switched on the lights for us better to see the wall painting, and opened the visitors' book for us to sign, and made us feel altogether welcome before slipping away. We felt warm towards that beautiful little church.

You can visit Baunton and Bagendon, North Cerney and Rendcomb, driving northwards up the valley, in an afternoon, and even on a midsummer Saturday, see scarcely a soul, though the main road will be busy enough.

It was an afternoon of tranquillity and sunshine, much needed after the chill of the ghostly morning, an extraordinary day of contrasts, of mood, of weather, of landscape, of atmosphere, and all within no more than a dozen Cotswold miles.

Stone in the Cotswolds

(Left) *The stone wall of Winson churchyard with a barn across the road. Note the early morning spider's web in the churchyard gate. There are many lovely dovecotes in the Cotswolds;* (below) *Georgian dovecote at Daglingworth;* (opposite bottom) *gable dovecotes at Duntisbourne Leer and Quenington.* (Opposite top) *Cottage roofs and gables in Winchcombe*

11. The Coln Valley

As I've written already, the Cotswolds suffer from the combustion engine. Some of the more popular villages and market towns will die of traffic thrombosis within the next decade unless something drastic is done, but a few places have been given their bypasses and are uncongested and unpolluted once more. And to anyone who has travelled in the region over the last twenty years, the most noticeable and dramatic improvement has been in Northleach. I used to drive regularly from Dorset to Warwickshire and the main road went right through the heart of the town. Now there is an unobtrusive and efficient bypass. Motorists can speed on their way without having to join the snail's queue, while Northleach is pleasant to walk about in, and doubtless to live in, once more.

I have read in several books about the Cotswolds that Northleach is a disappointment, a dull little place with none of the glory of Chipping Campden, Burford, Broadway. If it were not for the church, some imply, it would scarcely be worth a visit.

I find that quite extraordinary. Certainly the charms of Northleach do not seduce you at first glance; it is plain, even a little bare, there is no obvious prettiness or lushness about it. But it has some of the nicest houses in the area, set on all sides of the market square and in all the lanes running downhill around and

The River Coln near Yanworth; (right) *St Peter and St Paul, Northleach*

behind it; houses with good, elegant façades, and in enough variety of sizes and periods to be interesting, not dully uniform.

Go down one of the little lanes that slope away from the market square, and when you reach the level, turn and look back. Then you see the church in its greatest glory, it sails above you like a ship, its marvellous tower rising up out of the nave, as dominating as that of Chipping Campden – though not, finally, so soaringly, romantically celestial.

I think you would have to live in Northleach, get to know it quietly over some years, before its true character

emerged. But I remember how welcoming I found it one morning in summer when the town was *en fête*. It was still early, the sky was misty and grey, the day didn't promise well for outdoor celebrations. In the square, they were setting up stalls and the oven for a pig roast, and at the far end was a lorry with a long trailer surmounted by a canvas awning. On the trailer was a band, the men already resplendent in maroon jackets, and their conductor – a lady, heavily pregnant. There weren't many people about, but the band entertained us, nevertheless, with the kind of catchy tunes brass bands play, and the square came alive, everyone looked suddenly cheerful as they went about their work.

And as I was about to leave, they struck up 'Spread A Little Happiness', and for two pins, I could have danced all around the square. I didn't, only went on my way singing and feeling good, about the band and the fête day, and about Northleach, and the wonderfully unlikely things that suddenly happen in an English market place.

Not far from Northleach, a mile or so along the Fosse Way, is Fossebridge and here a little road takes you down one of the most delightful valleys in the whole of the Cotswolds – the valley of the pretty River Coln, that runs down through the villages that take its name – Coln St Dennis, Coln Rogers, Coln St Aldwyns, passes through Bibury, flows towards Fairford.

The best thing to do is wander with it, for in this whole valley there are delights everywhere you look, sloping meadows, tucked-away cottages, sudden perspectives of roofs, of groups of trees, of water glimpsed as it runs over stones, under bridges; there are horses and stable yards, barns, farms, manor houses, small churches, tombs – nothing in the smaller villages stands out as being especially rare or striking or unusual, and really, that is the whole point. It is the quiet

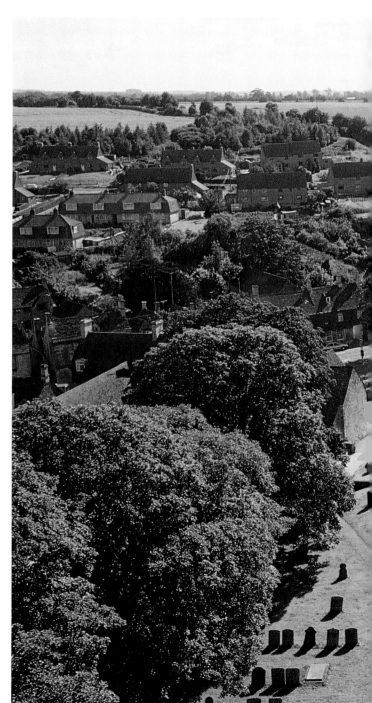

Northleach from the church tower

harmony of this part of the Cotswolds that gives such pleasure; the unobtrusive blend of stone houses into the landscape, the way the light touches a weathervane, the sight of a row of plant pots full of white geraniums balanced on a dry stone wall, a cat basking in the sun on steps leading up to the loft above a hay-barn, a hunter whinnying as it pricks its ears and smells the air, the drift of smoke from a garden bonfire pungent and nostalgic in the nostrils, sunflowers in a row.

Walk about these villages, and you will find your own particular corner, your own favourite view, the house you'd like to own, the most welcoming church.

The small village of Winson is not one of the best known in the Cotswolds, yet it seems to me to have as well as anywhere else that spirit that is suddenly, instantly recognisable. It has a tiny Norman church and a steeply sloping churchyard with some of the finest tabletop tombs in an area which is rich in them

The Coln Valley near Yanworth

indeed, and when you stand beside the wall over the lane, look left to see a perfect house, the classical façade of an eighteenth-century manor, with nothing whatsoever out of place or a single jarring note. What is not more than a path runs around the back of the main lane; here you can see the strips of the vegetable gardens, the old stone privies, the backs of cottages which are not as neat as the fronts but more homely, a donkey in a field, a rabbit hutch – once upon a time every back garden would have had its pig in the stone stye, too.

From Winson, to Ablington which is a bit grander with its imposing sixteenth-century manor, and Ablington House, and an air of lordliness and gentility but there is nothing unwelcoming here – it's always hard to put a finger on exactly why one small village has a different feel from that of its neighbour a couple of miles away. It has to do with the size of the houses but, I think, more to do with style and the trappings of domestic life, with small details of decoration as well as with the sweep of a driveway or the smartness and

Winson: (above) *St Michael's church with* (below) *tabletop tombs in the churchyard*

(Opposite) *Ablington House;* (below) *the River Coln at Ablington*

freshness of paintwork, with what people grow in their gardens, and whether a barn is used for hay, or is being converted into an expensive house.

Ablington is built around a sharp bend in the River Coln. After that, it curves gently and delightfully as a wave in a girl's hair, until it arrives at one of the more familiar of Cotswold place-names – Bibury.

I last went to Bibury very early on a bitterly cold, bright morning at the end of January. I had only ever been previously in spring and summer, and had been dismayed at how much traffic there was, how many cars were lined up along the street, how many people milled about beside the stream and up the lanes beside the famous Arlington Row. Another place spoiled by its own success, it seemed, and I wished it were not so, for Bibury is very special, it has a particular character similar to that of other famous Cotswold places, yet is quite distinctive.

On that January Sunday morning, there was no one else in Bibury at all – scarcely, it seemed, anyone else in the world. I had the village to myself, and saw at last how very beautiful it is, with the river running through, and the bridge over, and the grey stone houses.

I sat beside the water, well-wrapped against the cold, and fed bits of crust to the eager ducks; there aren't many activities more innocent and happy than duck-feeding like this. But after a while, it really was too cold to sit and I walked the whole length of the village, following the line of the street, towards the church. During the week, cars and lorries hurtle through between eight and nine in the morning, en route for

Cirencester or Burford, but on Sunday, no one. From the ivy-covered Swan Hotel crept the smell of frying bacon, hot coffee – it was wonderfully quiet.

It's very hard to get a new eye on famous places which have become so familiar in photographs, not to feel that they are over-exposed, over-praised. Arlington Row is preserved with care; it belongs, now, to the National Trust. And it is very, very pretty. The cottages in their perfect row climbing the lane are text-book models of Cotswold cottages but you cannot do other than admire and enjoy them – especially when

Early morning: the River Coln at Ablington

Bibury: (above) *Arlington Row which belongs to the National Trust and is one of the most popular places in the Cotswolds;* (right) *Bibury church*

you are doing so without the company of dozens of others.

In the lanes that climb up behind Arlington Row, there are other cottages, and newer houses, too, set behind nice gardens, and more breakfasts were cooking, but still I did not see a soul.

I went down to the church. This is the best corner of Bibury. The dark woods that lie behind the village were bare, and a thousand rooks flew up, from a thousand nests high in the tree tops, cawing and crying.

The churchyard, enclosed, well-kempt, lies close to the river. Follow it a little way, and the path brings

you into the grounds of Bibury Court, once home of the Sackville family and now a hotel. Walking here, I thought again about how water lends life and personality to a place, how pleasurable it is simply to stand and watch the flow of it over the stones, and hope to see a fish deep in the cold, clear water.

The trees are marvellous here, and because I like winter trees, I was as happy in January as when they are thickly in leaf, and giving deep shade to the lanes and paths and cottages.

Across the grass, Bibury Court stood, a stately, many gabled Jacobean manor house, towering and

Looking across the River Coln to the village of Coln St Aldwyns

rather austere. The January wind cut across the open space, and ruffled up the surface of the River Coln. I walked back more briskly, and met a few early church-goers, muffled against the cold. Above Bibury, the blue of the sky had clouded over, with low-bellied iron-grey snow clouds. By the time I reached the car, the first thin flakes were blowing on the wind; I had had the best of the day. And the best of Bibury.

South and east of Bibury, the Coln valley becomes even lusher; this is flat, sweet, gentle countryside, sheltered and fertile. After the bleak, bare, upland villages of the Cotswolds further north, it may seem tame, and too prettified. Perhaps it is, and I don't think I would want to live in this part of the Coln valley for very long. But I spent a particularly happy summer there, twenty years ago, and so it lies happily in the memory.

A clerical family I knew had gone to do a holiday *locum* in the vicarage at Coln St Aldwyns, which also took in the parishes of Quenington and Hatherop. I went to stay with them, during August. I was writing a book, and I had a bedroom overlooking the vicarage lawn, and across the valley to the river beyond. Every morning, I worked at a table in the window – so that in my mind, the book is forever bound up with that peaceful, sheltered, friendly place.

It was a hot summer and the afternoons were drowsy, the trees had lost their freshness, and the leaves hung heavy and very still. There seemed to be no air until the freshness of later evening came – as is usual in a river valley. I used to walk along the flat road out of the village to the bridge, and take the path through the water meadows, and sit there sleepily, watching the insects jazz upon the surface of the water, or listening for the plop of a water vole. Otherwise, the countryside did not stir in the heat of the day.

In the evenings, the family and I played endless games of croquet on the vicarage lawn and were still playing until we could no longer see to drive the balls

(Above) *Coln St Aldwyns;* (below) *tabletop tombs in Quenington churchyard*

through the hoops. Then we gave up and walked down the lane to the pub.

On Sunday mornings, I often went in to the early Communion service to which only a handful of people came. The church is next to the vicarage, reached by a side path directly from it, and in the early morning, it was cool and smelled of the damp and stone and dust of hundreds of years compressed together, the smell of every village church in the Cotswolds.

Later, I sometimes drove the visiting vicar to take his service at Hatherop Castle, or at Quenington and went for walks through the fields, explored the villages while I waited to bring him back, and it was always so utterly quiet. There might have been no one in the world on those brilliant summer mornings except me and, occasionally, a rabbit.

Quenington has one or two remarkable things. Not one but two magnificent, carved stone tympanums over the church's two doorways, perhaps the best in the Cotswolds. Over the south doorway is depicted the Coronation of the Virgin, with the symbols of the four evangelists – an angel, an eagle, a lion, a bull. Over the north door is Christ in triumph over Satan and Death, with a sun shining above, in which is hidden the face of God the Father. Near to the Church of St Swithin is a gatehouse which once formed part of the buildings belonging, from the twelfth century, to the community of Knights Hospitallers.

Back to Coln St Aldwyns, across the parkland and the green, green valley, back to breakfast, and then sitting reading Dickens in a deckchair under the trees, and the wasps dancing in ecstasy over the first few fallen plums.

It was, in retrospect, a perfect and a quintessentially

The tympanums at St Swithin's church, Quenington

The post office at Coln St Aldwyns

English summer. A year ago, I went back, a thing I often say I will never do, for time deceives, memory cheats, places alter, the past can never be returned to. But Coln St Aldwyns had not changed – though there were a few brash new stone-faced houses, and when I peeped in through the side door of the vicarage, the lawn was smaller than I remembered. Things always are. But the pretty almshouses were the same, the bean poles, the straight rows of sweet williams and the flower baskets might have been the very ones; and the same cottages clustered around the green, and the same lane led to the same cheerful pub in which we had drunk cider and played darts and been young together that happy summer.

I was glad, for once, that I had gone back.

To the east of the River Coln, and flowing in a similar, parallel course to it, is the River Leach: they join up, and flow together into the Thames, south of Lechlade. And the low-land of the Leach has a group of villages with three remarkable churches.

Eastleach Martin and Eastleach Turville are separated by two hundred and fifty yards, and a little flat stone bridge over the water. Stand here, and half close your eyes, and you can very easily imagine a summer's afternoon a hundred or so years ago, when small barefoot boys lay on their stomachs on the bank and tickled for trout, or sat dangling their legs in the water, and held fishing rods made from twigs and string and pins – the sort of setting, the sort of scene, painted by a hundred sentimental Victorian water colourists.

I have never been here, even in the middle of the season, and found more than a couple of other people about, and the churches have always been empty.

Eastleach Martin is a redundant church now, kept clean and full of flowers, but not used for services. Eastleach Turville has a saddle-back tower, and both are set off by the woods behind, and the green, green water-meadows, and the glitter of the stream as it courses over the stones, and both are best from outside, unremarkable within.

To the east of the River Leach lies an area through which run all manner of streams and brooks, like a network of veins flowing towards the River Thames. It isn't a particularly interesting part of the Cotswolds scenically, but it's worth making a detour for the village of Filkins – once on the main Burford to Lechlade road but now, mercifully, by-passed and happily islanded again. Not only is Filkins a particularly beautiful village with every cottage and house, barn and old privy made out of the local Oxfordshire stone, but it has had a new life breathed into it and is full of small but thriving craft workshops and galleries – a pottery, furniture restorers, a stone mason, cane and rush workers and, largest of all, the Cotswold woollen

(Opposite top) *The church at Eastleach Martin and* (bottom) *the clapper bridge over the River Leach.* (Below) *The craft workshops at Filkins*

weavers who work from a great converted stone barn, all in a complex of farm buildings and stables set around a grassy court. If the Cotswolds have for centuries meant sheep and woollen cloth, here they still do.

It's a region which grows more and more conscious of its past, and efforts to revive and celebrate aspects of it are being made proudly in many towns and villages. At Filkins, there is an exhibition which explains the part that sheep and the wool industry have always played, and there is cloth, wool and garments for sale.

(Below) *The font in St Peter, Southrop and* (opposite) *the herringbone-patterned wall*

Interior of the barn at Southrop

minor road takes you through the village of Southrop, on the Leach, and Southrop is to be visited for its church which contains a carved stone font equalling that at Rendcomb. Amongst other carvings set in recessed panels are the virtues overcoming the vices, and an elaborate formal border-pattern runs all around above them.

Outside the church, the stone walls are unusually set here and there in a herringbone pattern: go round to the back, and you find more of it. The churchyard is especially grassy and has the feeling of an old orchard, and the air is rich with the smell of fresh manure, from the midden on the other side of the high stone wall. Go around the wall, and ahead of you, along one side of a handsome farmyard, is the most magnificent barn, swept bare now – you can walk in and look up at the ribs of the roof, and know what Jonah felt like in the belly of the whale.

And so to Fairford. It has a High Street on a smaller scale than Cirencester and Chipping Norton but reminiscent of both, with the same classical eighteenth-century elegance and restraint to the houses, the plain façades, set on four sides of a rectangle. Beyond, at the top, lie the water-meadows of the river Coln, giving a lightness and airiness to the main design of the town.

But although Fairford has one of the nicest Cotswold streets, and a refreshing absence of tourist-catering, it is for the Church of St Mary that you come here.

'John Tame built the fair new church at Fairford, and his son, Sir Edmund, finished it,' wrote Henry VIII's chaplain, John Leland. John Tame made his fortune from the wool trade, was alive when Fairford Church was consecrated in 1497, but died three years later. (His son, Sir Edmund, also rebuilt St Peter's at Rendcomb.)

Whilst other men built magnificent churches in the region, no one else endowed one with stained glass to rival that of St Mary's. There are twenty-eight windows, all around the church, and the glass in them is un-

The only serious drawback to visiting this otherwise industrious but, on the surface, peaceful corner of the Oxfordshire Cotswolds is the appalling noise from innumerable training aircraft flying low from RAF Brize Norton a few miles away. They are a forcible and unpleasant reminder that the tranquillity of present-day country life is – at least partly – an illusion.

From Filkins, it's a straight road to the last of the market towns on this south-eastern edge of the Cotswolds – Lechlade. It *is* Cotswold in feel, and there are some good eighteenth-century houses, and a large wool church, but Lechlade suffers badly from sitting bang at the junction of two major roads.

If you want to enjoy a smaller, quieter market square, go from Filkins south-west to Fairford. The

touched, undamaged, unrestored since 1500 – with the exception of the west window which was blown in by a great gale in 1703, and replaced.

There is much magnificent church architecture in the Cotswolds. There are treasures of stone carving, tympanums, fonts, gargoyles, of carving on rood screens and pulpits and bench ends, marvellously preserved wall paintings, pieces of embroidery, monuments, tombs. Many things interest, speak quietly to the spirit, prompt reverence, awe, delight. But I do not know of anything that takes the breath away, that is so intensely moving, artistically and spiritually, that uplifts and enlightens the soul, as that stained glass at Fairford. Walk slowly around, with the excellent and very clear booklet about the windows that you can buy at the door. You will learn as much about the Christian faith, the gospel story, the parables, the mysteries, the drama of it all, as from reading the Bible, listening to sermons, being taught by priests. No one could come away unmoved, or fail to be made to think deeply, to question, to puzzle, to respond.

The beauty of the glass is, like the beauty of all the greatest art, quite extraordinarily *fresh* – it could have been finished yesterday, it looks timeless – *of* its time and yet modern, too. The colours sing, they are deep deep sea blues and greens, the ruddy brown of the Cotswold earth, the sharp acid green of apples, vermilion, scarlet, sun yellow, colours that have not faded or lost their brilliance.

You can spend an hour here, looking, thinking, letting the glass speak to you, and it feels like a few minutes, and when you go outside again, into the Cotswold daylight, the world looks different somehow, you see it through the eyes of the men who made the glass, and the colours of things leap out at you.

There is simply nothing like it in the region, nothing so intensely beautiful and expressive. And standing there, as it has for almost four hundred years, quietly in a corner of the everyday market place, open and free for all to enjoy and learn to love and live by, time after

Windows in the church of St Mary in Fairford. (Above) *Eve takes the forbidden fruit; and the burning bush.* (Right) *The risen Lord visits His mother on Easter morning; and the holy women are met by the Lord*

time. It would be worth coming from the other side of the world, just for this. I daresay many people do.

A few things change you when you have once seen or otherwise experienced them – teach you, inspire you, take you one step further on in understanding, alter your view of the world, so that you are never the same person again. I have not felt such a change within me so strongly for a long time, as I felt the day I came and saw the glass at Fairford.

12. Painswick

Bisley – Miserden – Sheepscombe – Painswick – the Slad valley

I have left the best until last although perhaps 'the best' in the Cotswolds, as in anything else, remains finally no more than a matter of very personal opinion. There may be a general consensus of agreement about certain individual buildings of great beauty and distinction, and the charm of a dozen Cotswold villages is obvious, but why I feel so strongly drawn to this last corner, why I respond to it, why its slopes and folds and small streets sing to me the most special song of all, does not perhaps admit of any clear explanation or justification. Other people may not agree with me, and will choose their own vista, their own favourite village, and church and walk and vantage point, whether high on the uplands or in the valleys, among the well-known names or along secret and private by-ways.

The journey to my own best beloved corner of the Cotswolds begins unassumingly enough at Bisley, a delightful, large village set on steep slopes, a few miles to the east of Stroud. Whenever I have been to Bisley, I have come away with a memory of roofs – for it is built on so many levels that in every direction you look up, or across, or downhill, and see a wonderful assortment of them, all aslant. Climb up the path towards the church, turn, and look back across to the small row of cottages on the opposite hill. They rise in a line, looking for all the world like a terrace of railway cottages, or back-to-backs in some old northern industrial town. They have an L. S. Lowry touch about them. If you cross the main village street and go up the snicket that brings you out on the level with them, you discover that they have some of the best kept, most traditional-looking kitchen gardens in the county, modest but perfect examples of their kind. Set side by side, they are long and narrow and not an inch of precious growing space is wasted.

Bisley is a bit of a rabbit warren of a village, dropping steeply down to where seven springs spout water out into the Bisley wells, and climbing up again to right and left, a village full of beautifully proportioned yet higgledy-piggledy cottages and houses, with the unexpectedly handsome or quaint or odd discovered on every corner.

From Bisley we go north on a road sweetly named Calf Way, through pleasant, open, high but not particularly remarkable countryside. After a few miles, it is worth making a slight detour, across to the village of Miserden. This is a small, undisturbed sort of place, with wonderful views across to the thick wedge of trees on the far side of Misarden Park, and a church in which are three surprising and delightful tombs with recumbent marble effigies on top of them. There they lie, these lords and their ladies of the seventeenth century, very straight, very graceful in their repose,

Painswick from Bull's Cross; (right) *looking down from the lych-gate outside All Saints church, Bisley*

Bisley. (Opposite) *The cottages and their vegetable gardens;* (top) *ducks at the wells and* (above) *a wonderful display of Cotswold roofs*

hands together in prayer, faces grave and calm; the little figures of all their sons and daughters are lined up around the base of the tombs and, touchingly, those who died in childhood and infancy are granted a special and separate place.

Retrace your steps and cross the Calf Way, and take the signposts pointing in a westerly direction, to Sheepscombe. Sheepscombe was a weavers' village, and the whole is so spread and scattered across the slopes that rise up to the magnificent thick woods that it is more like a district than a single village.

But whatever you call it, Sheepscombe is lovely, and although there are a lot of relatively new cottages in amongst the old, nothing obtrudes, the overall impression is good, and there is so much space, so much green space, in between. In autumn, it is especially beautiful here, as it is too at Cranham, a few miles to the north, a village on a ridge overlooking even more dense and spectacular woods opposite. Indeed, this is one of the most thickly wooded areas of the whole Cotswold region. The mature oaks, beeches, limes and ash trees grow great and fine and tall in their thousands, and lie like the pelt of some animal over the backs of the hills.

To drive from the Sheepscombe valley up to Cranham is a very roundabout and contrary way of getting to Painswick, but I think that is the best way of approaching the town. This is partly because the woods lining the high road are so beautiful, partly because you can stop at several points on the steep A.46, get out and after climbing onto the open ground, feel like a king surveying the world for mile after mile around, an exhilarating, dramatic thing to do, especially if the wind is blowing and tossing the tree tops about, and the clouds are scudding over the Severn plain.

(Opposite top) *Miserden;* (bottom) *a February landscape near Sheepscombe*

The Butcher's Arms, Sheepscombe

If you arrive in Painswick from this direction you do so by the main road that cuts through the top end of the town, but although they would be better off without the A.46, especially in summer, it does not spoil all, or even the best of the place.

When I first went to this westerly Cotswold town, I knew only the name on the map, it was an area I had not visited. I had no idea what Painswick would be like, whether I would be surprised, disappointed, or unimpressed. I did not expect it to be a place that would captivate me so completely, and at once, for it to become unquestionably my most loved Cotswold place.

It was the end of December, a couple of days after Christmas. Painswick was very quiet, there were no visitors at all and most of the residents were tucked up inside their cottages. The weather was awful, grey, cold, drizzling. We parked the car beside the church, just off the main road and began to stroll about, to try and get the feel of the place. We wandered down steep lanes, around corners, through little alleys. Where curtains had been left open, lamps glowed, fires burned, and in every window, a Christmas tree, magical with fairy lights in the darkening afternoon.

Away from the lanes, the wind blew soft rain into

Painswick: (above) *façades in the high street and* (left) *Friday Street*

our faces from the valley and the slope that rose up beyond it. There was that moist, sweet smell borne on the wind, of winter earth and fallen leaves; we couldn't see anything of the countryside now, only stand and smell it and know that it was there.

The next morning, we awoke to brilliant sunshine in a frosty blue sky, and to the bare line of trees fringing the ridge away beyond our top floor window. In Painswick, as in so many other Cotswold places, the green fields come right up to the door.

We went out again, to walk through the narrow hilly streets in daylight, and see perfection at every turn. I had wondered if my delight of the previous evening had merely to do with the prettiness and welcome of Christmas and all the Dickensian attraction of small cottage rooms lit from within. No. Painswick in daylight had me in thrall: the soft greyness of the stone (it was Painswick stone with which they built Gloucester

Cathedral), the plain, graceful lines of the seventeenth- and eighteenth-century houses, the pleasure of so many windows, doorways, absolutely right for their setting. Painswick is a town of hidden houses, of coming round corners and finding the unexpected.

And the church is marvellous, with a beautiful, silvery spire and the extraordinary avenue of clipped yew trees and table-top tombs for which it is so famous. Inside, all is light and airy and spacious.

That second evening, returning to Painswick after an afternoon in the countryside around, we went for a walk in the churchyard, and half the blackbirds of Gloucestershire were there too, darting low in and out of the yews, squabbling, crying little warning cries, finally singing their evening song, so that they were

Yew trees and tabletop tombs in Painswick churchyard

somehow more than mere birds, they became the spirits of the place.

Walk down the steep lanes and you reach the stream that runs along the bottom of the Painswick valley. After that, you climb away uphill again, and then, from the other side, you can look back across to where Painswick lies peaceful, and safely spread, its church spire drawing your eye in towards itself, and then away, to the hills that rise up far behind. It is a setting similar to that of Chipping Campden, equally right and satisfying to behold.

I have been back to Painswick several times since that first winter weekend, but I have not been in the summer. People tell me not to do so, that the lanes are choked with cars, the main road in a permanent roar, the town almost as full of tourists as Broadway.

So I shall always go there in late autumn and early spring, and best of all, at Christmas time, when the lanes are quiet and the trees on the ridge stand bare, and the lamps are lit in all the welcoming windows of Painswick.

My Cotswold journey has brought me finally to a valley I knew by heart and in every lovely, loving detail long, long before I ever saw it, a place I first read about nearly thirty years ago and have dreamed of ever after.

I wonder if the people of Slad, past and present, mind very much that their village and their valley have been immortalised, have become a part of the inner lives, the imaginations, of so many thousands of souls – not to mention whether they mind all the pilgrims who beat a path to their doorstep.

Laurie Lee's autobiography of his Cotswold childhood in the years immediately after the First World War, *Cider with Rosie*, is a book I know almost by heart; I love it as I have loved only perhaps twenty

Painswick from Bull's Cross

books or so in my lifetime, intimately, defensively and joyfully. It is a perfect celebration of the past of rural England, evocative, sunlit, spilling over with life, it describes a time and a way of life long vanished, a country world which can never return.

I wondered if it also described a place that had changed for the worse, and had been spoiled forever, or at least whether the Slad valley would bear no relation to the Slad of Laurie Lee's golden memory and lyrical description. I went there almost reluctantly;

View down the Slad Valley towards Stroud

perhaps after all it would be better to stay away, to keep the book and what it meant to me untouched by reality.

But oh joy that I did, and joy indeed that I need not have worried, for I found a place so beautiful, so perfect in itself, and in many ways so faithful to the book that I have been back again and again and each time felt more sure. I have returned to the book again, too, and re-discovered it fresher and richer and all the better for knowing the real place.

For what after all *could* ruin Slad, or alter it very much? You cannot alter the lie of the meadows or the shape of the valley itself, the view down it, the feel of it

Looking towards The Camp from Slad

all. They could be allowed to build too many new houses, but I suspect that planning permission would be withheld; trees will die or be felled in time, but others will be planted to take their place. Slad is not the Slad of fifty years ago, socially or economically, but in many, many ways, it has not changed: the snow still falls and the earth lies hard as iron in the grip of the Cotswold winter, the cow parsley still grows tall in spring, and the willow-herb in summer. There are days in July and August when the valley lies still and hazy under the heat, and the gardens are, as they were then, 'dizzy with scent and bees'.

I have stood in the lane that runs beneath Swift's Hill to the east of the village, stood at a gap in the beeches that line it, and gazed down over Slad and felt that rare, unmistakable sense of absolute rightness and contentment that only comes in a few places, a few times in a life, a peacefulness, a rare, rare silence of the spirit. It is gentle countryside, undulating, feminine,

View towards Bull's Cross from Swift's Hill, in the Slad Valley

green, the long valley sweeping down and away towards Stroud, the meadow slopes nearer at hand rising and falling, one upon one, soft as breaths. The individual trees, the hedgerows of hawthorn, the steep slopes of the beeches that climb up and round, the high ground curved like a full breast, and the stone houses set about here, and here, and here – all these contribute to the final beauty and yet individually they are not in any way exceptional. As so often in the Cotswolds, the whole of the Slad valley is far, far more than the sum of its parts, every detail is right, every element modest, none dominant.

I know more spectacular bits of the Cotswolds, more famous, more obviously pretty, but I know nowhere that gives me such complete joy, that is quite so flawless, and yet real, living, not artificially preserved. I think I could end my days in this little valley as contentedly as anywhere on earth. Each time I go back to it, I wonder fearfully if the spell will work, if I was right after all. Each time, it does, and I know for certain that I was.

On my last visit, I stood again at my spot between the beech trees on that high, narrow road, looking across the meadows and away down the valley, remembering with joy the book that had brought me here and the debt I owed to it. And all of a sudden, the sun came out between the clouds, and flooded all the fields with lemon-coloured light that came rippling up towards me in wave after wave as the branches of the trees shifted about, and I knew that for certain, in this magic spot, I had found what I had been looking for, the place where the pure spirit of the Cotswolds bubbled up out of the ground like a spring. And I knew that it would always be here for me to drink deep and be refreshed, renewed, restored.

My journey was at an end.

Index

Bold entries indicate the main entry;
italic indicates an illustration